GUIDE TO
FISHING

ROB BEATTIE

© Haynes Publishing 2018
Published June 2018

A CIP Catalogue record for this book
is available from the British Library.

ISBN: 978 1 78521 244 4

Library of Congress control no. 2018932891

Published by Haynes Publishing,
Sparkford, Yeovil, Somerset BA22 7JJ
Tel: 01963 440635
Int. tel: +44 1963 440635
Website: www.haynes.com

Printed in Malaysia.

Bluffer's Guide®, Bluffer's® and Bluff Your Way®
are registered trademarks.

Series Editor: David Allsop.
Front cover illustration by Alan Capel.

CONTENTS

"Hell, if I'd jumped on all the dames I'm supposed to have jumped on, I'd have had no time to go fishing."

Clark Gable

GONE FISHING

There's a fishing scene in the 1936 screwball comedy classic *Libeled Lady* when leading man William Powell (whose character has clearly never held a fishing rod in his life) emerges from the last of many dunkings to discover that he's caught – by purest fluke – the biggest trout in the river. Standing there under the admiring gaze of Myrna Loy (the object of his affections and the reason he's soaked) and her fishing-obsessed father (once disapproving, now looking on with newfound respect), he watches as his just-purchased copy of *Trout Fishing for Beginners* floats down the river behind them both before rounding a bend and disappearing out of sight. His secret safe, Powell, beaming, responds to their praise with a modest: 'It was nothing.'

This is Olympic-standard bluffing and, although you can't expect to start at this sort of level, over the course of *The Bluffer's Guide to Fishing* you'll learn everything you need to know to hold your own among the enormous and diverse angling community – whether it's in a cosy snug over a pint of old Chubthumper, on board the

Saucy Sue for a day's mackerel fishing with a can of supermarket lager, tipping down a peppered vodka on Russia's Kola Peninsula or enjoying a bracing glass of 12-year-old McBeattie with a dash of water as the mist rises over the Spey.

With any luck, you'll never need to get your feet wet, but if you do, help is at hand.

The Bluffer's Guide to Fishing will go a-angling (there's a reference to Izaak Walton, the godfather of fishing writing) so that you don't have to. It will help you to tell your pinkies from your gozzers, your boilies from your pop-ups, PVA bags from bait droppers, bite alarms from buzzers, Hairy Marys from March Browns, and ragworms from lugworms. It will take you inside the secretive world of the specimen hunter, open the Aladdin's Cave of carp angling and the rapacious multimillion-pound industry that rides on its scaly coat-tails, eavesdrop on the sepia-tinted stuck-in-the-50s world of salmon anglers and their gillies, strike out in search of Mongolia's mighty taimen (minus the inconvenient bear attacks) and introduce household names like John Wilson, Chris Yates and Big Girl the carp, all from the comfort of your armchair.

Throughout this book the words 'fishing' and 'angling' will be used interchangeably and, generally speaking, this is perfectly acceptable. It is done all the time, as you will shortly discover. However, once you've mastered some of the basics, you will probably find yourself discussing 'fishing' with fellow anglers and 'angling' with those who don't fish. It's a small and seemingly contradictory point but, as every bluffer knows, the devil is in the detail. You should also know that the terms 'angling' and 'angler' are very rarely used when talking about 'game' fishing. Confused? Don't worry; all will become clear over the next few chapters.

And remember, commercial fishing is entirely different from the sort of recreational fishing described in these pages. Well, strictly, it isn't – because they're both about catching fish. But that's where the similarities end. You, as a bluffer, will be pitting your estimable wits against a fish of very little brain with just a rod and a line, something tantalising on a hook, and sometimes a landing net. If you think that it won't be much of a contest, you're in for a very big surprise.

Fishing is a maze. People have spent lifetimes trying to find their way through it, and even a way out of it. The bluffer hasn't got a lifetime to spare, so when you find yourself on the spot, this short but definitive guide offers invaluable help.

It sets out to conduct you through the main danger zones encountered in discussions about fishing and to equip you with the vocabulary and evasive technique that will minimise the risk of being rumbled as a bluffer. It will give you a few easy-to-learn hints and techniques that might even allow you to be accepted as a fishing expert of rare ability and experience. But it will do more. It will give you the tools to impress legions of marvelling listeners with your knowledge and insight – without anyone discovering that, until you read this, you probably didn't know the difference between a fruit fly and a flash damsel.

"Angling or float fishing I can only compare to a stick and a string, with a worm at one end and a fool at the other."

Samuel Johnson

WELL AND TRULY HOOKED

The Irish literary critic Vivian Mercier once wrote of Samuel Beckett's absurd masterpiece, *Waiting for Godot*, that it 'has achieved a theoretical impossibility – a play in which nothing happens, that yet keeps audiences glued to their seats. What's more, since the second act is a subtly different reprise of the first, he has written a play in which nothing happens, twice.' This astute observation can equally be applied to fishing – with knobs on – since it is often a sport in which nothing happens, all the time.

Given angling's reputation for tedium, the bluffer must have a ready answer to the question perpetually posed by non-anglers, which may be paraphrased thus: 'Why on earth do you enjoy sitting outdoors in all weather, looking miserable and not catching anything?'

While the following answers might be suggested as jumping-off points, you should feel free to improvise as necessary. Since all anglers are characterised as congenital liars, bluffers have a unique advantage when describing their love of, and adventures in, fishing.

'IT GETS ME OUT OF THE HOUSE'

Since many people still hanker for life to be a version of a 1970s sitcom where the blundering or browbeaten husband is undermined and ridiculed at every turn by his shrewish yet domineering wife, this is a useful explanation that even now holds water. The stereotypes may have disappeared from the light-entertainment schedules, but they're still alive and kicking in virtually every family-oriented advert where women are clever, kind and resourceful, and men are well-meaning boneheads. Other anglers will usually respond with a look of rueful recognition.

'IT'S THE PEACE AND QUIET'

This response has a much more modern vibe and implies a certain thoughtfulness, as if still waters might actually run deep – and that there might be more to fishing than catching fish. Indeed, since most people have short attention spans when it comes to fishing, it is strongly suggested that you keep this little gem up your sleeve and practise delivering it like this: 'Why do I go? It's hard to explain.' Make brief eye contact, then look away wistfully into the middle distance and repeat: 'Let's just say there's more to fishing than catching fish.' Ooh, aren't you mysterious?

'IT'S THE HUNTER IN ME'

There's a school of thought which argues that one of fishing's primary attractions is that it taps into the need to feel that you're somehow connected to your distant hunter-

few odds and ends from the tackle shop, use bread and sweetcorn for bait, and go fishing in the sea.

5. Anglers support the economy

While you can go fishing on the cheap, no one really wants to. Not when there are rods named after hunter-killer submarines and reels so powerfully geared that two turns will bring in 30 feet of line and a perplexed-looking scuba diver. Anyway, who doesn't want a Kevlar fly rod so light that it's barely visible; or a bivvy tent that blends predator-like into the background so well that passers-by keep walking into it by mistake; or a beachcaster rod that can hurl a five-ounce lead 150 yards?

> "Fishing isn't a sport.
> It's a condition".
>
> *Anon*

---

6. Angling teaches optimism

You can't go fishing and not be an optimist, really. The odds are so stacked against the average angler – picking a day when the weather conditions are right; finding the fish in all that water; not scaring them off when you arrive (that's assuming no one else scared them off before you arrived); choosing the right method and tactics; convincing a fish to take the bait; playing the fish correctly, landing it, unhooking it safely; and then (sometimes) returning it gently to the water – it's a miracle anyone ever catches anything.

7. Fishing brings you closer to Nature

True. In an increasingly mad world, angling offers a rare opportunity to sit and stop and really see your surroundings. Good animals to mention in this context include muntjac deer ('Its haunches were so much higher than its withers') and mink ('Freed by animal activists? Not so, old chap; they've been breeding in the wild since '56, you know').

8. Anglers are conservationists

Bizarrely true, partly because they pay an annual licence fee which goes towards the upkeep of the waterways, and partly because they spend many hours repairing fences and stiles, keeping access paths open, trimming back banks and overhanging trees, removing excess weeds, and stocking waters with new fish – which in turn helps to promote a healthy ecosystem.

9. You can eat what you catch

Sometimes. Although the majority of the fish caught in the UK are returned to the water (what our American cousins call 'catch-and-release'), there are many fish that are really good to eat: trout and salmon, of course, and plenty of sea fish like bass, cod, pollock, whiting, mackerel and so on. But if the local rules allow, you can also eat small pike of around five pounds – called 'jacks' or 'jack pike' – as well as freshwater eels. There are other edible coarse fish, including perch and carp, but eating these is generally frowned upon.

10. Fishing takes you back to your childhood

This is a potent reason, and one that will often convince when all others fail. It's an opportunity for you to go all misty-eyed and recall entirely fictitious trips with old Uncle So-and-so, the fish you caught together, and the larks you enjoyed. Insert a few jam sandwiches, the odd flask of cocoa – as well as the occasional flight from an angry farmer's bull – and that's it, audience convinced, job done.

THE PRACTICALITIES

You can't, however, just go fishing whenever and wherever you like, because, like any activity that makes money for someone, somewhere, there are rules – mainly to do with licences and permits. These need to be addressed before you get on with the important stuff.

Fishing licences

You don't need a licence to go sea fishing, but in order to fish most lakes and rivers in the UK you'll need one (which allows you to fish in principle) and a permit or day ticket (which allows you to fish a particular stretch of water on a particular day or over a period of time). Generally speaking, you must have both of these bits of paper; one without the other is no good. You'll need to know that different rules apply in England and Wales, Scotland and Northern Ireland.

Fishing seasons

Sea anglers can fish whenever they like and are some of the sporting world's hardiest souls, if only because a beach in winter can be a miserable place. Coarse anglers can generally fish whenever they like throughout the UK, though there may be some local restrictions imposed by whoever owns the fishing rights. In England, you cannot fish rivers, streams and drains between 15 March and 15 June inclusive – because it's England, and they do things differently there – but you can fish for coarse fish, eels, rainbow trout and brown trout on most enclosed still waters and canals all year. It's all infernally complicated, so the best advice is to check locally before setting off on a fishing trip. And the best advice is not to be found in Byzantine local by-laws, but in your favourite fishing emporium – the local tackle shop. (Don't forget to buy something if you drop in. It's rude not to.)

TYPES OF FISHING

There are four different kinds of fishing that you should become familiar with.

Coarse fishing
This is the most popular style of fishing in the UK, and can be practised on pretty much any kind of water – stream, river, canal, drain, pond and lake. Why 'coarse' fishing? It's said that the term became widely used in the late nineteenth century by the landed gentry who preferred to fish for trout and salmon – these fish were considered 'game' (like grouse or pheasant) while other kinds were dismissed as 'coarse'. The term has stuck. Coarse-fishing methods include float fishing, ledgering,

spinning and free-lining. Popular coarse fish include carp, roach, tench and bream.

Game fishing

Although traditionally more expensive and exclusive than coarse fishing, game fishing for trout and salmon has become increasingly popular in recent years – partly because of the business that's grown up around purpose-built lakes stocked with large trout, and partly because holidays to places where fish are plentiful – like Canada, New Zealand, Russia and South America – have become more affordable. Game-fishing methods include fly fishing and spinning. Popular game fish in the UK include brown trout, rainbow trout, sea trout (a type of brown trout known as 'sewin') and salmon.

Sea fishing

There's been a resurgence of interest in sea fishing spurred on by readily available, cheap day trips, as well as the popularity of the whole foraging, self-sufficiency fad. Fishing on or off the coast of the UK can be pretty grim but, equally, it can be a thrilling and rewarding experience. Sea-fishing methods include ledgering, spinning and float fishing. Popular sea fish include mackerel, cod, bass, whiting, flatfish and pouting (and they can pout better than a trout).

Faraway fishing

Affordable fishing holidays to exotic destinations such as Russia, Mongolia, New Zealand, Canada, Argentina and the Caribbean have transformed what used be a niche style of angling into more of a mainstream pursuit. All popular techniques from the other branches of fishing apply; it's just that what's on the other end of the line may be 10 or 20 times the size and has likely been hit really hard with the ugly stick. Note that this is sometimes known as 'sport' or 'big-game' fishing. If the subject comes up, always seek an opportunity to mention Ernest Hemingway's *The Old Man and the Sea,* his memorable fable about an old man, a young boy and a giant fish. If you feel like coming over all lyrical, say softly: 'My big fish must be somewhere.' (Don't elucidate.)

TYPES OF WATER

Unless you have a rich, landowning friend who has a lake or pond or river, buying a licence is only half the story. Once you have permission to go fishing, you then need to get permission to fish a particular spot; sadly for anglers, this involves putting your hand in your pocket.

Day-ticket waters

Anyone can fish these, usually for less than a tenner a day. Bluffers can pretend to be fans of such places and refer to them as 'commercial fisheries', as in: 'I know commercial fisheries are easy but I find them useful when I'm experimenting with a new bait or tactic.' Alternatively, feel free to be rather snooty and dismiss them as 'carp puddles' (many such lakes are shallow and stocked with small carp) in a sentence like: 'Yeah, but it's a carp puddle, isn't it? I just don't get it – there's no challenge.'

Club waters

The fishing rights and access to these are owned by angling clubs or societies; a single club may own the rights to a dozen or more lakes and ponds, as well as stretches of river. Note that it's common for different clubs to share the same stretch of river, with each one having access to only one of the banks. You pay an annual fee which allows you to fish any of the waters 'owned' by your club; expect to pay anything between about £60 and £100 per year for the privilege.

There are so many different types of water and styles of fishing that it's easy for bluffers to cover their tracks. Use phrases like 'It's a hard-as-nails water but that's the challenge,' or 'I prefer a family-friendly fishery,' or 'They may be unfashionable, but I think that bleak [a type of coarse fish] are beautiful.' Real anglers will read between the lines, as follows: 'Everyone fishes for the same three enormous catfish,' 'It's stuffed with tiny F1 carp', and 'The otters have eaten everything else.'

Syndicate waters

These are like club waters but more exclusive, more expensive and much more secretive. For example, while clubs are always trying to boost their numbers, syndicates rarely advertise openly for new members. Instead, they snare you on the sly, maybe over dinner or at a rugby match, with whispered tales of enormous, rarely-fished-for specimen carp; of how you're 'their' kind of angler; of how you'll have to meet some of the members at a tiny, out-of-the-way pub and convince someone else to second you; and how it's expensive but worth it. It's a bit like joining a secret society, minus the horrid initiation ceremony (you hope) – though, if asked, say you're allergic to chicken's bottoms. Syndicates are the bluffer's friend since no one expects you to talk about them; just nod mysteriously and, when asked about the fishing, shake your head as if in wonder and laugh lightly.

Private waters

The Holy Grail. Believe it or not, there still remain some waters (especially small ponds and old estate lakes) that are rarely fished or may never have been fished at all. It's every angler's dream to track down one of these mysterious beauties and get permission from the owner to enter piscatorial paradise. Some result in utter disappointment because, by herself, Nature is a lazy mistress, just as likely to stuff a pond full of tiny roach and perch as to sprinkle in a few record-breaking rudd and crucian carp. So private waters are pot luck and, like syndicates, meat and drink to the bluffer because, again, no one expects you to discuss any of the details. In other words, feel free to be as vague as you like and then mime pulling a zip across your lips. If you want to push your luck, say something like: 'Johnny Brockhampton and I go back a long way, and once a year a gang of us get together at his family trout pond. Good water. By invitation only, I'm afraid.'

Free waters

The dregs. Waters so hopeless, so overfished, so 'family-friendly' that no self-respecting angler would go near them unless utterly down on his or her luck. Litter-strewn, overrun with gangs of kids hanging around or tooling up, dog walkers with their hated balls and – the angler's true nemesis – canoeists slipping past with noses that are both up in the air and sneering at the same time. The bluffer can pour scorn on gratis fishing with one exception: always mention the free stretch of the River Stour to the south-west of Ringwood in Hampshire which, if you go upstream of the famous Throop Fishery, still holds a good head of chub, roach, barbel and pike. Your angling cred will inch up another notch.

THE SEX ISSUE

According to a survey by the Environment Agency in 2001, only 5% of anglers in the UK are women which, unsurprisingly, means that anglers are overwhelmingly blokes. Thus, heterosexual male bluffers in search of someone to impress over a glass of Pinot with their knowledge of, say, the mating habits of *Anguilla anguilla*, the common eel, may have to endure more blanks than red-letter days. Still, bluffers may turn even this to their advantage, since given angling's lack of ladies' appeal, apparent interest in the subject is actually an excellent barometer of their interest in you. Just wash your hands first.

Finally, if this all seems a bit much to take in, the bluffer can be consoled thus: it has been said that a fishing rod is a stick with a worm at one end and a fool at the other. In other words, other people aren't expecting very much from you in the first place. So, if in doubt, simply remember your training and repeat after us (*sotto voce misterioso*): 'There's more to fishing than catching fish.'

Big-game anglers really do have that leathery, sun-ravaged, Hemingway-like skin, and look like they should be on the set of **Thunderball**, *drinking a Mount Gay rum and soda.*

cold conditions may put the fish off, they won't deter the serious angler. They're forever coming up with new tactics and techniques, and if you find them busily note taking in a meeting, they're just as likely to be sketching out a new rig as they are crunching that quarter's sales figures.

The key here is that it is the fishing itself that holds the appeal, with the size and species involved only a secondary consideration. The serious angler knows all about barometric pressure, the significance of wind direction and air temperature, and is able to 'read' the water like the rest of us read a magazine.

THE TROPHY ANGLER

In days gone by, trophy anglers might well have been called 'specimen hunters' and they certainly share many of the same characteristics. They're just as passionate and knowledgeable as serious anglers but have a fascination for a particular species of fish which they will pursue at any cost – personal and financial – until they have caught one that will be recognised by their fellows as a specimen; only then will they be able to move on to the next species. Thus, a trophy angler may spend years chasing a giant perch at the expense of all other fish, travelling far and wide in the search for a monster, reading all the literature, and trying all manner of exotic baits and tactics in his or her effort to land the fish of dreams. Then again, because it's all about catching the fish, if the trophy angler is fortunate enough to catch it at the first attempt, there's no loyalty left to that particular species; instead, he or she will tick it off the list (oh yes, trophy anglers have lists) and move on to the next one immediately.

> "It has always been my private conviction that any man who pits his intelligence against a fish and loses has it coming."
>
> *John Steinbeck*

Trophy anglers are relentless. If they've reached the part of the list that says 'p' for 'pike', they won't be distracted by anything so frivolous as a trip to Russia's famed Kola Peninsula in search of monstrous sea trout, or the chance of trotting a famous English chalk stream in the winter months for giant roach. Nope, they'll keep on, *Terminator*-like, dragging their weary bodies across the fishing world's terrain until their goal is achieved – at which point they'll drop said fish like a hot potato and move on to the next one. Relentless and fickle, trophy anglers are the most driven of all angling's brothers.

THE TRADITIONAL ANGLER

Traditional anglers can barely muster any interest in fishing as it is done today but, when it comes to how it used to be, are hardly able to restrain themselves. Expect to find them enthusing over a manky old bob float that most anglers would chuck out of their tackle box in a heartbeat, running a gnarled hand down the length of a creaking cane rod so warped you can barely get a line through its rings, or setting a centrepin reel spinning in the palm of their hand and making you stand there watching it as it whizzes round and round and round interminably, all the time intoning: 'Look at that, you don't get engineering like that these days.'

Traditional anglers prefer rivers (because most modern anglers don't), small ponds and out-of-the-way lakes. They love going to Ireland or to those funny counties in the middle of England that aren't quite the South and definitely aren't in the North – like Shropshire or Lincolnshire – where they can disappear in a fog of pipe tobacco and gorge themselves on toasted tea cakes and pints of Old Scrote.

THE BIG-GAME ANGLER

Remember the 'It's-the-hunter-in-me' explanation for going fishing in the previous chapter? Big-game anglers can say that with a straight face, since it's possible that the fish they catch will weigh many times more than they do. There's something about catching a fish that's bigger than you that moves angling away from being a whatever-it-is (sport, hobby, pastime, obsession?) and takes it firmly into the realms of hunting. There's a significant difference, however, because it's rather difficult to 'put a lion back' once you've caught it; and, while most people's idea of big-game fishing conjures up the image of an enormous, bloodied carcass strung up on the quay, these days most fish are returned alive – and perhaps tagged – to fight (and spawn) another day.

Big-game anglers fish in short bursts. You're unlikely to find them strapped to a fighting chair, man-against-fish, *Jaws*-style for hours on end. These days, the best advice is to match your tackle so that it's possible to land a fish quickly and efficiently without exhausting it.

With that preconception punctured, it's time to confirm another one: yes, big-game anglers really do have that leathery, sun-ravaged, Hemingway-like skin, and look like they should be on the set of *Thunderball*, drinking a Mount Gay rum and soda.

THE CRUELTY QUESTION

It's inevitable that bluffers will find themselves confronted by an angry person claiming that fishing is cruel and enquiring how you'd like it if someone put a hook in that canapé and then dragged you across the room and up the stairs before ripping it out of your mouth and chucking you back over the banisters and down into the party to wander around with a big gash in your mouth? They'll then look at you in smug satisfaction as if no one's ever thought of that analogy before, while they await your response.

Well, you can't very well put your hands up and plead guilty as charged, since that will blow your cover with any experienced anglers in the vicinity. Instead, try the following, depending on which way you lean in real life.

Ask your accuser if they know the difference between fishing for food and fishing for sport. If their jaws hang open uncomprehendingly, give them a brief appraisal of 'game' and 'coarse' fishing as described in the previous chapter. As far as the former is concerned, you generally only return a fish to water if it's considered too small to eat or fish stocks are low. Otherwise you 'dispatch' it, as swiftly and humanely as you can, and eat it later. Regarding the latter, your argument might go as follows:

You do not rip the hook out of a fish's mouth and then chuck it back in the water. These days, most anglers use barbless hooks which are very easy to slide out and cause very little damage. Second, fish are returned gently to the water; the angler usually cradles a fish until it actually swims away, thus ensuring that it has recovered from the exertion of the fight. A fish is often unhooked still inside a landing net which is then lowered back into the water so that it can meander off in its own time. Anglers handle small fish with wet hands or a damp cloth to minimise any damage, and large ones are kept safe on padded unhooking mats where they can be liberally doused in water while being unhooked.

Do fish feel pain? Nobody knows except the fish, and the science changes almost every time a new study comes out. In February 2003, for example, the *Daily Telegraph* reported the findings of James D Rose, a professor of zoology and physiology at the University of Wyoming in the USA, who concluded, 'Pain is predicated on awareness,' adding that awareness of pain depends on functions of regions of the cerebral cortex which fish do not possess. Two months later, the same newspaper carried a story on studies conducted by Dr Lynne Sneddon from the Roslin Institute near Edinburgh which concluded that rainbow trout do feel pain. 'We found 58 receptors located on the face and head of the rainbow trout,' she said, pointing out that these nociceptors respond preferentially to tissue-damaging stimuli. The RSPCA dismissed the first study but accepted the second.

If you're genuinely conflicted about it – and some anglers are – then argue that it's about balance. Point out the good that anglers do by caring for lakes and rivers and the wildlife that live there by dragging unscrupulous polluters through the courts to make them pay for fouling waterways (point out that government's role in this is patchy at best, pitiful at worst); by pumping money into the local economy (tackle shops, B&Bs, club memberships and so on); and by keeping would-be tearaways off the streets so they're minding their own business in the middle of nowhere instead of stealing the lead off your roof or running a set of keys down the side of your car.

Remind critics that you use only barbless hooks which are easy to remove, that you match your tackle to the size of the fish so that you're less likely to suffer a line break, that you set your tackle up such that if the line does snap, the fish isn't dragging around a float or weights that can easily become tangled and kill it, that you tire fish properly before banking them so they don't flop about and hurt themselves, that you use an unhooking mat or leave them in the landing net, and that fish are never 'chucked back', but returned gently to the water to fight another day.

One final point: anglers often find themselves on the wrong side of an argument, particularly when it comes to animals that the public loves or admires. Otters are always dangerous territory (blame Henry Williamson, author of the touching but terribly misleading *Tarka the Otter*) but the bluffer should stand firm. Otters are fearsome predators of fish and will often kill in that joyful and sadistic Tiggerish way, only to leave most of the carcass to rot. They also range for miles and can decimate fish populations, especially if they get into a small fishery unnoticed. Cormorants are even worse and, whereas in the 1960s and 1970s about 2,000 of them settled in the UK for the winter, that number has risen to 23,000, according to the Angling Trust. Given that each bird scoffs around one pound of fish a day, that's 4,000 tonnes a year down the swanny.

Walking into a fly- or game-fishing shop without any money is like trying to gatecrash Oxford University's infamous Bullingdon Club; they look at you like you've just carried in a dog turd on the sole of your shoe.

TALKING TACKLE

In order to convince others of your love of all things angling, you will need to learn a little about the tools of the trade – or 'tackle' as it's more widely known. Note that this word plays to the Brits' enduring love of the double entendre, and any enquiries along the lines of 'So, how's the old tackle holding up?' should be greeted with a weary sigh and a resigned look that says 'Ha, ha, yes, very funny.' (Reward a persistent offender by sneaking out to his car and tipping half a pint of maggots into the boot; these will wriggle off obligingly and insert themselves into the tiniest of spaces, becoming invisible in a few moments. Give them a week or so to pupate and after that, when the wag opens the car door, he'll be greeted by a swarm of angry bluebottles – *Omen*-style. He'll never be able to prove a thing.)

The different types of angling will be explained in more detail in the following chapters, but for now all you need to know is that all fishing tackle can be broken down into the following constituent parts:

Rods The long, whippy things that are slightly thicker at the end you hold and thinner at the end nearest the fish.

Poles Even longer whippy things with the same characteristics as rods.

Reels Spools that are used to store, retrieve and release the line; most reels hold hundreds of yards of line.

End tackle The different bits and bobs (like floats, weights and hooks) that are attached to the end of the line furthest away from the angler.

Bait Tempting morsels attached to the end tackle (sometimes, but not always, hooked) designed to trick fish into biting.

Everything else Clothes, bags, waders, bivvies (little tents), umbrellas, chairs, bedchairs, bite alarms, fish finders, bait boats…As you'll discover, it's easy for an angler to end up with an impressive amount of tackle. (Don't even think about it.)

RODS

Unfortunately for the bluffer, there are dozens of different types of fishing rods – feeder rods, waggler rods, Avon rods, Avon/quiver rods, carp and pike rods, spinning rods, jerkbait rods, boat rods, beachcasters, ledger rods, float rods, fly rods, salmon rods, split-cane rods, spod rods, stalking rods, match rods, feeder/combi rods…you get the idea. But rather than delve into each – and waste time that could be better spent on more interesting things like wine, golf and skiing (all subjects expertly covered by *Bluffer's Guides*) – they will be broken down into a few easy-to-remember categories.

Before that, it's worth noting that every rod has a few things in common with its bedfellows. Namely:

Construction

Most modern rods are made of carbon fibre; some are Kevlar. Rods your dad used were probably made of fibreglass, and some fly rods might have been split cane, in which case they might be worth up to £1,000 if they were made by the famous Northumbrian manufacturer Hardy. (Always claim that modern fly-fishing rods don't have quite the same 'action' as a vintage Hardy 'Palakona'.)

Action

This describes the bend of the rod when you hook a fish. Tip-action rods remain more or less straight but bend at the top; progressive-action rods start bending about two-thirds of the way down; while through-action rods bend all the way through – you can feel them bending through the handle. (Rod nomenclature has to be this simple or anglers won't understand it.)

Reel 'seat'

All rods include a way of securing the reel to the handle – either two rings which are just pushed into position or a pair set with a thread which are screwed to keep the reel in place.

Rod rings

Rings attached to the rod at intervals through which the line is threaded; they're typically bigger near the butt and smaller towards the top.

As observed before, there are far too many rods for bluffers to memorise, so here are a few key types to get you through most angling situations:

Rods named after the fish they're designed to catch

These are easy. It's perfectly acceptable to talk about a carp rod, pike rod, bass rod, flattie (flatfish) rod or salmon rod, or even a barbel rod; this won't raise any suspicions with either fellow anglers or tackle-shop owners. Rods for carp, pike and barbel typically come in two pieces and are about 12ft long; salmon rods usually range from 12ft to 14ft and will probably come in two or three pieces. However many pieces a rod comes in, they are always tapered. Just remember that the thickest part is nearest you, and the thinnest part nearer the fish.

Avon/quiver rods

These are essentially two rods in one. Basic models come in three sections: the butt section, which is the thicker end that you hold and has a handle usually made of cork and/or neoprene with either two rings or a screw thread to attach the reel, and two top sections. The first of these is styled to match the butt section and gets progressively thinner towards the tip; this is mainly used for float fishing. The second of these has the same aerodynamic shape but the end is finished in white and then topped with a much thinner, brightly coloured and much more bendy tip – the 'quiver' tip – which is used for ledgering. More expensive Avon/quiver rods will include a variety of coloured tips and some include a separate extender section to increase their length by two feet. (Note: it's called an Avon/quiver rod because early versions were developed specifically to fish the fast-flowing River Avon – the one in Hampshire, as opposed to those in Bristol and Bath, and the Midlands.)

Feeder rods

These are basically like Avon/quiver rods without the Avon bit. In other words, they only come with top sections that are quiver tips. They'll often have multiple tips – some heavy, some light – which are designed for coping with fish of different weights or for different types of water (a light tip isn't so good for fishing a big powerful river, for example, because you'll spend all your time thinking you've got a bite). They're also sometimes called 'quiver tip rods' or 'ledger rods'. Feeder rods can be anything between 9ft 6in and 15ft long.

Waggler rods

These are also like Avon/quiver rods, but without the quiver bit, and are designed for float fishing. They usually come in two or three sections and are typically between 11ft and 15ft long.

Spinning rods

Short rods of between 7ft and 10ft designed to cast metal, rubber or plastic lures. The Yanks have recently muscled in on this particular act with their baitcasting rods where the reel sits on top of the rod, as opposed to underneath it. Like many real anglers, the bluffer should feel free to describe this arrangement as newfangled and unnatural.

Poles

The odd-one-out in that you don't use a reel with a pole. Instead, it's basically a really long rod that is 'shipped out' over the water by adding sections until the tip is directly over the point you want to fish; you always use a float with a pole, attached to the end via an elasticated contraption which helps take the strain when you hook a fish. Although most pole anglers fish between 11m and 13m out from the bank, you should buy one slightly longer – between 14.5m and 16m. Because you're a bluffer.

Fly rods

As we'll discover, those who fly fish are something of a breed apart (*see* page 71), but there are some simple generalities that'll come in useful. Most anglers agree, for example, that a 9ft fly rod for 5-weight line is a good general purpose combo. The weight of the line is important, and the right choice will underline your bluffing credentials. Overloading a rod with a heavier line than it's designed for, can cause it to break; under-loading it can make casting next to impossible.

Bluffers should note that there's an easy way to tell a fly rod from other types: the reel seat is right at the bottom of the butt rather than near the top. This allows you to hold the rod correctly for casting and controlling the line. Since proper fly anglers often don't use the reel for playing a fish (*see* 'The Play's the Thing', page 76), almost any fly reel will do.

Boat rods

If this were *The Lord of the Rings*, then the short and stocky boat rod would be Gimli the dwarf. Boat rods are specified by length, followed by the breaking strain of the line they're rated to use. Thus a typical boat rod would be between 6ft and 8ft and graded to fish with line of between 20lb and 50lb – for example, 7ft (20lb to 40lb). But for really big fish, the breaking strain of 'braid' line can go from 80lb to 130lb (or more) and the rod handle can be nearly as thick as your wrist.

Beachcasters

Ah, if only all angling was this straightforward. Yes, these rods are designed to cast baits from the beach, which means they're usually 12ft or longer and powerfully constructed so as to sling relatively heavy weights – say, 4oz to 6oz – without snapping in half.

"There he stands, draped in more equipment than a telephone lineman, trying to outwit an organism with a brain no bigger than a breadcrumb, and getting licked in the process."
(Paul O'Neil, LIFE magazine)

REELS

Fortunately, there are only five main types of fishing reel which between them are used for every kind of angling. They are:

1. **The centrepin reel** A drum with a handle that revolves on a central spindle.

2. **The fixed spool reel** Takes the centrepin, makes it deeper, turns it 90 degrees and then fixes it on a geared spindle. The line is then wrapped onto the spool via a rotating bale arm.

3. **The multiplier reel** Takes the centrepin, makes it fatter and then winds line onto it via a geared handle.

4. **The baitcaster reel** Like a miniature multiplier.

5. **The fly reel** Like a little centrepin.

You don't need to know how any of these work; simply be aware of their names.

END TACKLE

This is the stuff that goes on the end of the line and ends up in the water. Bluffers who've walked their dogs by a local lake, sat outside a river pub, enjoyed a trip to the seaside or watched Robson Green bellowing his head off on Channel 5 may think they have a passing acquaintance with basic end tackle – a float, perhaps some weights, a hook, a lure or a fly. You will, however, be utterly unprepared for the bewildering array of other ingenious bits and bobs that can take their place on the other end of a typical angler's line. Here are a few examples to whet your appetite: bait that's made of plastic; hooks that don't go into the bait; sliding floats that can be fished at any depth; bags of bait that can be attached to the end of the line and then dissolve when they come into contact with water; coloured wool; radio-controlled model boats which can ferry tackle into places that would be impossible to cast to; and stealth rods that disappear when you're not looking. (Note: one of these is not a real item of tackle.)

BAIT

Bait can be neatly divided into several basic types. There are baits that are pleasant to use like bread, sweetcorn and cheese; baits that are unpleasant to use like maggots and worms; and baits that are beyond unpleasant like slugs, ragworms and trout paste. Finally, there are Frankenstein baits called 'boilies' that were invented in a laboratory and include ingredients like acid casein and Antarctic krill. (Many anglers who couldn't even boil an egg are quite at home in the kitchen cooking up their own boilies. It's one of life's mysteries.)

EVERYTHING ELSE

Ah, how anglers like to surround themselves with stuff, so much so that it's not unusual to see one pushing a wheelbarrow piled high with boxes, bags, a chair, sleeping bag, kettle and other miscellaneous camping gear. And that's not including the tackle boxes with their disgorgers and baiting needles, swivels and clips, rubber tubes and bits of styrofoam, weighing scales, rod rests, landing nets, keepnets and more. The key elements are:

The tackle box
Many items of tackle – particularly floats – are surprisingly flimsy and must be protected, so anglers usually have a box (rather like a plastic DIY-style toolbox) to hold everything. Inside this may be several smaller boxes – one for hooks, another for weights and so on – so that the whole thing resembles a matryoshka doll. Fly anglers will have one or more fly boxes, while sea anglers carry everything around in buckets.

Landing nets and keepnets
While small fish can be swung out of the water and straight into your hand, all anglers pine after fish that are too big for this – hence the landing net. Essentially, it's a net on the end of an extending pole that's used at the end of the fight to land larger fish safely. Keep nets are like really, really deep landing nets attached to a much shorter pole. The pole is driven into the bank and fish are popped into the net as they're caught so they can be admired altogether at the end of the day before being returned to the water (or weighed if you're fishing in a competitive match).

Rod rests

Essentially a sharp metal pole which is driven into the bank, it has a V-shaped attachment at the top on which the rod is rested so that it lies horizontally. Some are really complicated and highly adjustable, but they all serve more or less the same purpose – and allow the exhausted angler to have a bit of a snooze after carrying all that tackle around.

Chairs and bedchairs

Most anglers need somewhere to park their behinds. Typically, a chair will have individually adjustable legs to cope with uneven banks and will err on the sturdy side. Bedchairs have a seat long enough to let you lie down and have a proper kip.

Bivvies

Small, domed tents, favoured by anglers who are fishing a long 'session' – usually over a single night, but sometimes over several if they've been kicked out by a long-suffering spouse or partner. This takes angling into the realms of camping and requires extra equipment such as saucepans, stoves, cutlery, lamps, sleeping bags, pillows, perhaps a nice feather duvet...

So where does all this stuff come from? What marvellous, magical emporium is responsible for delivering these wonders into the eager hands of anglers of all descriptions? Prepare yourselves to enter a veritable cave of wonders – the Fishing Tackle Shop.

TACKLE SHOPS

Like most independent retailers, tackle shops have been hit hard, first by superstores – yes, there are angling superstores – then by mail-order companies, and finally by online stores. As a result, most larger towns may only have one or at most two tackle shops – those near the sea may have more – and these will have only moderate levels of stock and will charge higher prices. They're still important though, both as a source of local information about which venues are fishing well and as a supplier of certain types of bait – maggots, casters, worms, various frozen sea baits – for those who either don't have the stomach or the wherewithal to source their own. (Note that it's possible to buy bait online – yes, there is a website called Worms Direct – and also note that your postie may not thank you for it if said item is not properly packaged.)

Tackle-shop owners tend towards the chronically miserable, partly because of the aforementioned downturn in their fortunes and partly because the job seems to attract the same kind of characters who think that, just because they enjoy going to the pub, it would be a good idea to run one. This basic error – confusing the joy of handling a beautifully balanced fly rod and reel with trying to sell the same to a tight-fisted customer who, with a keen eye for a bargain, keeps quoting fictional websites and demanding to know if you'll price match them – is clearly visible behind the haunted expression of the tackle-shop owner.

If a bluffer should attempt to engage a tackle-shop owner in friendly conversation, the likely response will be a rebuff. There is no shoulder so cold as the one that's been repeatedly disappointed by tyre-kickers coming in, spending hours getting advice, trying every bedchair in the shop ('Ooh, this one's even comfier') and hefting various combinations of reels and rods ('Can I try the first one again?') before walking out with a packet of hooks and a free catalogue, going straight home and turning the computer on.

No, best not to bother. Instead, hang around outside the shop until one or two regulars have wandered in for their daily moan and maggots and then slip in behind them. Most tackle-shop owners feel strangely vulnerable if forced to move out from behind the counter, so as long as you don't catch anyone's eye, you should be left in peace. This will give you the chance to become acquainted with some of the more common brand names – Fox, Shakespeare, Mitchell, Daiwa, Leeda and Shimano – which you can drop casually into conversations at a later date.

"I should never make anything of a fisherman. I had not got sufficient imagination"

Jerome K. Jerome

There is an important exception to this all-tackle-shop-owners-are-cut-from-the-same-miserable-cloth rule. The tackle shop that specialises in fly or game fishing is an entirely different experience, more akin to an old-fashioned gentlemen's outfitters, where servile types gently lift the shoulders of expensive jackets to ensure they sit perfectly on your bowed shoulders or ask, as you're trying on some moleskins – with a commendably straight face – 'which way sir hangs'. In fact, going into a fly- or game-fishing shop with money in your pocket is a wonderful experience where you're made to feel part of an exclusive club that only the select few are allowed to join. By contrast, walking into a fly- or game-fishing shop without any money is like trying to gatecrash Oxford University's infamous Bullingdon Club; they can sense your lack of funds, look at you like you've just carried in a dog turd on the sole of your shoe, and force pleasantries out of pursed lips that would rather spit at you. Here, the only way out is to double bluff and pretend to be so wealthy that you a) don't need to know anything about angling – or anything else; and b) are so fabulously wealthy that you never carry any money on you, anyway. It takes platinum levels of bluffery to pull this off, but do it with enough chutzpah and you'll stand at least a chance.

If you're flush, it's always a good idea to patronise your local tackle shop. They are a dying breed and deserve your support – even if it's thin and unconvincing. Nothing thaws the cold heart of a tackle-shop owner more than a generously paying punter, and you'll find it useful to have someone in your corner if another customer challenges you on something or – God forbid – asks your advice.

PRACTISE, PRACTISE, PRACTISE

Finally, to avoid any glaring faux pas on your first day out on the bank, on the beach or on the boat, the bluffer should take time out to practise a few basic tricks and techniques.

1. Practise setting the reel up (this may involve unlocking the handle using a simple mechanism) and putting it on the rod, then refer to the instructions to open the bale arm, take the line and thread it through each of the eyes on the rod in turn.

2. Practise tying a hook onto the end of the line. Two reliable, easy-to-tie knots are the 'knotless knot' and the 'half-blood knot' (*see* illustration on page 51). Knots are a particular obsession of fly fishermen, so make sure you know your most basic perfection loop and reel knot.

3. Buy half a pint of maggots (the smallest amount) and put your hand into the box. Once you can let them wriggle all over your fingers without pulling your hand away or screaming, try picking one up between your finger and thumb. They're also apparently quite good at removing gangrenous tissue if you happen to have an open wound.

4. Still with us? Tie a size-16 hook onto your line and hook a maggot onto it. The idea is to nick the skin of the maggot near the thick end.

5. Can't bear it? Use the same technique with a piece of sweetcorn from a tin.

6. Take the rod and reel and a ledger weight of an ounce or so out to somewhere isolated and practise casting. Once you're tackled up, let about four feet of line out

so that the weight swings nicely beneath the rod tip. Then hold the rod with your preferred hand so that the first and second fingers are in front of the reel and the third and fourth fingers are behind it, and hook your first finger over the line. Open the bale arm and – still holding the line hooked with your finger – lift the rod up and over your shoulder and then bring it forward as if using a long-handled axe to split wood. When the rod is about 30 to 40 degrees above the surface of the water, unhook your finger to let go of the line and the motion of the rod will propel the weight forward. The first few times this will probably be horrible, but persevere and you'll soon get the hang of it.

7. Planning to go fly fishing? Turn to page 71 for a more detailed rundown of the pitfalls that lie in wait.

8. Finally, if you want to look the part, tie the end of the line to a handy armchair and then practise straining the rod against it as if you've got an enormous fish on the line. Throw a few shapes. One day soon, all this will be yours…

KNOTLESS KNOT

1

2

3

4

HALF-BLOOD KNOT

1

2

3

4

5

"Fishermen are born honest, but they get over it."

Ed Zern, *To Hell With Fishing*

REEL TIME

As you will recall, there are basically four different styles of fishing: coarse, game, sea and faraway/sport. The problem for the bluffer is that each of these categories have myriad variations which lie in wait, ready to trap the unwary into a giving-the-game-away schoolboy error.

Obviously it's impossible to go into all that: first, because it's mind-blowingly unending; and second, because it defeats the purpose of this book, which is to get the bluffer in and then out of the fishing world with the same amount of effort as that expended by a fat trout in a stocked lake (a 'stockie' – you can have that piece of jargon for free) as it rises lazily to sip a mayfly from the surface.

With that in mind, how is the bluffer to know that saying 'Caught my biggest-ever mirror carp, fishing proper old-school – bolt rig, method mix – on the far bank. Get in, you beauty,' will raise not a glimmer of interest (except perhaps because of the rubbish street *patois*); yet this: 'Best way for bonefish is to long trot with double caster, feeding plenty of hemp to start, then

53

a handful of pinkies every other cast,' will set listeners to stroking their chins and making little ear-pulling signs to each other?

The chapters that follow reveal the secrets to bluffing about very different types of fishing, honed over the years and designed to extract the maximum amount of credibility with the minimum amount of effort. Prepare to go out on focused fishing trips using the advice in each of the four chosen disciplines so that you understand something about the steps involved – where to go, when to go, some planning, more than a few tactics, and a bit about the mechanics of casting, catching, playing, landing and releasing – and then, most importantly of all, bragging about it in the pub afterwards.

THE ART OF
COARSE FISHING

WHEN TO GO

You can catch coarse fish all year round, though some species are more associated with specific seasons. Thus you should know that rudd and tench are often at their best in summer, chub and pike in winter, perch and barbel in autumn; many fish like carp, bream and roach feed happily all year round. Freshwater eels can be a nuisance in spring and summer when they'll take baits meant for other, better-looking fish, and they are slippery swines to unhook.

On hot days, you'll do best in the early morning or evening and on into darkness. If you're trying to catch a fish from the surface (anglers get terribly excited by catching something they can see, as opposed to dropping the bait into water that looks like soup and hoping for the best), then you may do okay during the middle of a hot summer's day, as fish such as carp like to drift around just under the surface; however, the heat also makes them lethargic and disinclined to feed. In winter, you'll often do best in the middle of the day when the water has absorbed a bit of heat – otherwise, many species will just be holed up somewhere, dozing and minding their own business.

You should avoid windy days until you've mastered your tackle. It's extremely difficult to demonstrate your high level of expertise when your line and everything attached to it spends all day in a bush, up a tree, round the legs of your chair or attached to the collar of an excitable dog that's running away very quickly. A warm, overcast day provides the very best conditions for fishing; if you can go then, your chances are excellent.

WHERE TO GO

In the main, you'll have a choice between still and running water. Running water is always more difficult to fish because it moves. This may sound obvious, but you will find it harder to cope with everything associated with running water. Drop your float or ledger into the river in front of you and in moments it'll rocket off downstream before swinging round under your own bank, where it will either get snagged or rise up in the water and hang there, flapping next to the bank. Riverbanks are often steep and treacherous swims to fish (like other anglers, you can call any place to fish a 'swim'). Often harder to access, there's less room for you and your gear so it's more awkward to tackle up, control the tackle, hit a bite, land the fish and so on.

Instead, you'd be strongly advised to try your luck on a still water where everything will be much more relaxed. Preferably it will be one that's well-stocked (sometimes called a commercial fishery) that offers plenty of features – for example, bays and inlets, islands, gravel banks, lily pads and reed beds...that kind of thing. Such features attract fish because they often trap food or make a good natural home for insects and larvae, and they also make the long hours of inactivity more bearable because they're nice to look at. Still waters are usually closer to the car park, and their swims are more capacious (and thus more suited to the frame of the modern angler) and more comfortable with fewer natural obstructions. Still-water angling is more popular than river angling and therefore better resourced; it's not unusual, for example, for a popular commercial fishery to have a roadside-style café serving all-day gut-busting breakfasts, or a tackle shop where terminally disorganised anglers can pick up some bait.

WHICH BAIT?

Some coarse fish are more partial to certain baits than others, so this often depends on what you're hoping to catch. Perch, for example, like red worms; tench like sweetcorn; carp prefer highly flavoured baits called 'boilies'; most fish like bread; and all fish like maggots. For you to have the best chance of catching anything first time out and cementing your angling credentials, logic suggests that you choose maggots as bait. Buy these from a tackle shop either on the day or the night before. A pint will do for a day's fishing – less for a morning or evening session. Make sure that the tackle dealer puts plenty of maize in with them to stop them sweating – a bit of useful bluffing knowledge. Keep them in a shop-bought plastic bait box which has a snap-on lid with air holes in it. Leave the box outside overnight or – if you live alone – in the fridge. Maggots kept cold in a fridge will last three or four days easily; otherwise they'll start to go sweaty and begin to smell (or stink, actually) within a day or so, before turning into casters or pupae. Casters are an even better bait than maggots, but you will be disappointed to learn that they're even less pleasant to stick on a hook, thanks to their easily popped skins and gooey yellow insides.

WHICH ROD AND REEL?

Given that there are so many to choose from, you're advised to buy an Avon/quiver rod to start with, since this will suit nearly every occasion and sidestep the need to be more specific when choosing which rod best suits whatever you're trying to catch. Avoid using a pole at all costs unless you practise assiduously with it first. Although capable of presenting a bait perfectly under a tiny float balanced like a ballerina on glass, in the hands of a novice, poles are instantly transformed into something hideously unwieldy – like watching a drunk in full armour trying to thread a needle with a 15-metre lance.

WHICH PITCH?

On arrival, take a tour round the lake and look at the various 'pitches' (another term for swims), stopping to talk with anglers if any of the following apply:

- Their landing net is visibly wet. This means they've probably caught a fish recently.

- They have a keepnet staked out in the water. This means they may have something to put in it.

- They are wiping their hands on a cloth. This means they may have just put something in their keepnet (or that they've just done something unmentionable with a shovel and a toilet roll).

- They're staring murderously at the water in front of them with their rod held loosely in their hands, perhaps with slack line round their feet. They may have just lost a fish.

- They've issued an expletive. This means they may have just missed a bite.

Having done a recce round the lake and noted who seems to be catching fish and how, return and collect your tackle. You now have several choices. First, move in next to someone (in the next swim – not literally next to them) and fish there. Second, find a spot that looks like theirs and fish there. Third, find someone who's fishing in a way you think you can emulate, fish next to them and copy what they do. Or any combination of these. It's not elegant, but it works.

THE ACTUAL FISHING BIT

There are plenty of how-to guides available on news stands (angling magazines breed like worms in a wormery) or at your local library, so the details of tackling up need not concern bluffers here. Thus there remain only three simple mistakes to avoid if you're not to be immediately outed.

First, don't place your rod on the rod rest as if you're leaning it against a wall; rods should be as close to horizontal as possible, which may mean driving a long rod rest into the bank at an angle, pointing towards the water. Many experienced anglers use two rod rests and lay the rod on them like a spit on a barbecue.

Second, always position the reel towards the front of the rod butt. Some rods have a threaded reel seat which makes the decision for you, but others have two sliding rings which you can place anywhere along the length of the rod butt. First-timers are often tempted to position the rings – and thus the reel – in the middle. Don't.

Third, always hold the rod with two fingers wrapped round the butt in front of the reel and two fingers behind it. Never hold the rod with your hand positioned behind the reel, as this will give the game away. It's the famous dead giveaway which outed the bare-chested Vladimir Putin as a non-angling poseur.

That's it. You're now ready to catch your first fish.

RECOGNISING A BITE

Much of the following advice applies no matter what style of fishing you have chosen for bluffing purposes.

When a fish takes the bait, you will be required to recognise what's happening and then act on it. A howl of triumph is rarely to be advised. The canniness of a fish is not directly proportional to the size of its brain and, amazingly, they seem capable of outwitting the most sophisticated animals on the planet – i.e., anglers. Think how much easier, then, they'll find it to outfox the hapless bluffer. Fortunately, this book is here to hold your hand (but not the maggoty one, thanks).

FLOAT FISHING (*SEE* 'GLOSSARY')

- If the float suddenly vanishes, it's a bite.

- If the float bobs and then goes under, it's a bite.

- If the float moves deliberately across the surface, there's a good chance it's being pulled by something, so it's a bite. Just think of the opening sequence of *Jaws*.

- If the float lifts and lies flat on the surface, then a fish has picked up the bait and is also carrying the weight of the small shot nearest the hook, which is why the float lies flat. Oh, and it's a bite.

- If the float twitches as if it's being knocked, it's probably a fish bumping into the float or the line. Stupid fish.

LEDGERING (*SEE* 'GLOSSARY')

- If you're using a bite alarm and it goes off, it's probably a bite.

- If the rod tip pulls round, it's a bite.

- If the rod tip jerks or looks like it's being tugged, it's a bite; wait for a good, solid pull.

- If the rod starts to bend slowly, it may be a bite but it may be gunk drifting across the surface that's got caught on the line – check first.

SPINNING (*SEE* 'GLOSSARY')

If something hits the lure hard as you're retrieving it, it's a bite (anglers call this a 'take'). Takes on lures are pretty hard to miss, as the fish usually hook themselves and start pulling in the opposite direction. The first time it happens you will feel a tingle of excitement, and numerous methodological surveys show that a high proportion of people holding a rod are converted instantly into proper anglers and never look back. Apparently.

HOOKING AND PLAYING A FISH

Unless the bite is very fast, then simply lifting the rod with a firm motion until you feel resistance is normally enough to set the hook; inquisitive anglers who've had the misfortune to test the point of a hook with too much enthusiasm know how sharp they can be.

Once the fish is on, always try to keep the rod up – between about 60 and 70 degrees – and then bring it up to 80 degrees as the fish nears the bank. Beginners usually make the mistake of lowering the rod progressively during the course of the fight until, by the end, the rod is almost pointing at the fish. This puts all the strain on the line – which is fine if you're reeling in a two-ounce gudgeon, but no good at all if you've got a lively, 7lb carp on the other end. Let the rod absorb the strain; that's what it's there for.

Fish of six inches or less can be lifted out of the water and swung into your hand. Larger fish will need a net to get them in safely. When a bigger fish is tired, it'll lie flat just beneath the surface. Keep the rod up and sink the landing net in the water, then draw the fish over the net.

Never try to push the net at the fish because you'll spook it. Result? Much splashing about; fish gets new lease of life and tears off again; anglers either side of you shake their heads at your utter cluelessness and snigger. Save yourself the embarrassment and wait until the fish is clearly done and then net it as just described. Once it's in the net, take the bale arm off the reel and put the rod down. Don't worry if the end of the rod drops into the water; real anglers know that this doesn't matter.

If it's a large fish, don't lift it out of the water using the handle; instead, ship the net in hand-over-hand and then grab the rim with both hands and lift it out of the water. Take the net to an area of soft grass nearby or use an unhooking mat and lay the fish down.

UNHOOKING

There are three important considerations here:

1. Make sure you have both forceps and a 'disgorger' (a slender length of moulded plastic or pressed aluminium used to remove deeply embedded hooks safely and humanely) and practise using them at home; there are videos on YouTube that will help here. You never know. You might have no intention of getting this up-close-and-personal with a fish, but you could be called on to offer advice about how to unhook one.

2. Make sure you use barbless hooks because they're easier to remove.

3. Be decisive without being rough.

IDENTIFYING AND PHOTOGRAPHING YOUR FISH

There are far too many coarse fish in the UK to attempt to identify them individually and you can sidestep any species-related enquiries merely by describing something as a 'good fish'. If you're fishing a commercial fishery then anything you catch is likely to be a carp; these look like koi carp wearing drab *Columbo* overcoats. If what you catch is darker, rounder and evil-smelling, then it's probably a bream; if it's got a spiny dorsal fin, it's a perch; if it's long and thin with a nasty grin, then it's a pike; if it looks like an eel, then it's probably an eel. A useful catch-all for a smaller fish that you can't identify is to call it a 'hybrid'; fish are free with their favours and different types will often mate with each other.

Bluffers might think about enlisting the services of a person of diminutive stature to hold the fish, to give the impression that it is larger than it is.

When photographing your catch, there's only one thing to bear in mind: scale. Typically, a lone angler will photograph the fish with something next to it – perhaps a rod and reel or a float – so that you can tell how large it is. Bluffers should avoid this and might think instead about enlisting the services of a person of diminutive stature to hold the fish, to give the impression that it is larger than it is. If you're with someone else, get them to photograph you holding the fish – but make sure you hold it carefully in both hands away from your body and towards the camera. This simple trick will make it look much bigger than it really is. Or, if you're really determined to push your luck, you can always doctor your photographs with some editing software (but no bluffer worth their salt would stoop to such measures).

By the way, the myth of the angler coming home without having had a bite and dropping in at the local fishmonger only works for game and sea anglers, or if your partner isn't able to tell the difference between a trout and a tench (hint: one is sleek and delicious and the other is brown and slimy); you can't buy coarse fish to eat.

SOME BACKSTORY

But wait. Although you can bluff your way through a visit to a commercial fishery, there are many different kinds of waters and styles of fishing still to be mastered. So here is a selection of stories, hobbyhorses and famous fisheries that you can memorise in an attempt to plug the gaps.

FIVE STORIES YOU SHOULD KEEP UP YOUR SLEEVE

The savage take

What happened 'I'd baited up the swim and just cast out. I didn't even have time to put the rod on the rest before – BAM! – it was nearly pulled from my hands. It was a big bastard and it went deep and fast into the lilies and smashed me up. Never stood a chance. Killed the swim, too; didn't have another touch all day.'

What actually happened You over-cast and caught your tackle in the lilies. As you pulled enthusiastically to free it, the line snapped and the ledger weight flew past your ear, embedding itself in the tree behind you.

The red-letter day

What happened 'First cast, I caught a specimen roach, the next cast, another; it carried on that way for 45 minutes.

20 fish, all roach, all over a pound. Fantastic, a real red-letter day.'

What actually happened Nothing. Nada. Zip. Bugger all.

'I didn't think there was anything in there'
What happened 'It looked so unpromising – weedy, shallow and scummy. Looking at it, you wouldn't have thought there was much in there at all. But would you believe it, just as the light was fading I caught the most amazing rudd. Must have been nearly two pounds. It was in pristine condition; I don't think it had ever been caught.'

What actually happened You were right the first time; there wasn't anything in there.

Battle scars
What happened 'These? They're nothing. Just a few cuts and bruises from trying to get into that difficult swim over in the corner. I managed to slip down the bank and onto the sunken log, then wormed my way along until I could free-line a slug under the tree. Definitely worth it; caught an enormous chub.'

What actually happened You were sitting in an ancient gardening chair, trying to make a long cast. When the tackle got caught in the branches of the tree behind you, you gave an almighty yank but instead split the canvas of the seat and your arse dropped into the hole in the centre of the chair. As you struggled to pull yourself free, the chair tipped over, bouncing your face off the bank and spilling maggots all over you. Look, there's still one in your hair.

The monster pike
What happened 'I was reeling in a little 'un when this enormous pike – probably a 20-pounder or more – rolled up from the bottom and grabbed it. We fought to a standstill. He was so huge I could barely get him up to the surface and when I did, the brute sort of looked at me and then charged off, snapping the line. Lost the lot – fish and all.'

What actually happened While you were still trying to get the range, a bigger, better angler cast to it first and landed it successfully.

FIVE PLACES YOU MUST CLAIM TO HAVE FISHED
Given that genuine fishing trips are likely to be few and far between, it's important that you plug the gaps with imaginary adventures at real venues. Fortunately, there are plenty of places other anglers will have heard of but never fished; concentrate your fire here.

Redmire Pool
No longer the mecca for large carp it once was (stories from the 1960s and 1970s resemble a cross between the *Beano* and *Swallows and Amazons*), it's still a name that resonates with every coarse angler. You don't need to give away the location (on the border between England and Wales), and you don't have to have a fishy tale to

go with it, either; better anglers than you have blanked at Redmire. Just bang on about the history and the atmosphere. And don't forget to puzzle over how such a small lake can cast such a long shadow.

Royalty on the Hampshire Avon

The South's mightiest river and one of the most difficult to fish. Nevertheless, tell your tale – how you queued outside Davis's tackle shop to get your permit, waited for the car park to open, got your gear and, trembling with excitement, walked over Companion Bridge to the Royalty Fishery where you tackled up at the House Pool (add colour by observing that the boathouse could do with a lick of paint) and fished the morning without any luck. After lunch you moved on to Fiddler's West where you rolled a piece of luncheon meat down the river and caught a personal best barbel at 10lb 11oz.

River Wye

Beautiful, fast-flowing river which runs along the border between England and Wales. Famous for salmon as well as barbel and chub. Tell people you've found a spot where you can wade out into the middle and then trot a single caster on a size 16 down a gravel channel and the fish actually fight each other to take the bait. Feel free to complain about snobby book lovers at the nearby Hay Festival, and those bloody canoeists lowering the tone.

Norfolk Broads

Tackling up below Thurne Mouth on the River Bure and fishing with an open-ended feeder, even the bluffer would struggle not to catch bream – and quite large ones at that. Thus the Norfolk Broads have the advantage of being a venue that anglers have heard of and that, if pushed, you could actually fish in real life with a chance of success.

The Secret Lake

One of the joys of angling is that you're not necessarily expected to reveal the location of a good fishing spot for fear that other anglers will descend en masse and ruin it. Thus, you can speak in hushed tones of an historic estate lake that's hardly ever fished, and the enormous, ancient carp that live there, even more inbred than their owners, never seen a bait before, hard to catch but that didn't stop you…

GAME, NET AND CATCH

Bluffers are advised to familiarise themselves with the meaning of the particular discipline of the art known as 'game' or 'fly' fishing. Traditionally thought of as the gentleman's choice (or even gentlewoman's – the late Queen Mother was a keen exponent of the sport), 'game fishing', as it is known and practised in the British Isles, involves tying an artificial fly onto a gossamer thread of tapered 'leader', itself attached to a fly line, itself coiled around a fly reel, which will eventually coil itself around your feet.

The essential components of fly-fishing tackle haven't changed for centuries. Neither has the profile of the typical fly fisherman (or queen). Game fishing is almost exclusively the preserve of purists, especially those who like nothing better than stepping out in their chest waders into fast-moving water and falling over.

The essential difference between coarse and game fishing is that the latter frequently involves eating your catch, which almost always (but not exclusively) will be a freshwater or seawater fish like a trout or salmon, or even a 'sewin', the Welsh name for a 'sea trout', which starts life in a river and then heads out to the sea (this is useful bluffing knowledge). Another key difference is that the use of live bait is expressly forbidden, and you might as well hang up your rod now and scuttle off in disgrace if you plan to cast a freshly-baited line of wriggling invertebrates or colourful live insects. It's as bad as moving your ball in golf or signalling to your partner in bridge. It's simply not done.

In recent years it has become ever more common practice for fly fishermen to return a catch, as rivers, streams and lochs become progressively overfished, but there is no stigma involved in keeping and eating a fine specimen from a well-stocked and regularly replenished source.

Bluffers should also note that 'spinning' for trout and salmon (using an irresistibly glittering lure cast by a spinning rod) is no longer as commonplace as it once was, and is actually banned in many places. Attitudes have changed over the past 50 years, particularly among a new breed of fly fishermen who frown upon the increased risk of injury to smaller fish and consider it simply not the done thing.

WHEN AND WHERE TO GO

Although fly-fishing purists celebrate the spring as the best time to catch trout, the increased popularity of commercial trout fisheries, stocked with large, fast-growing rainbow trout, has diluted this tradition somewhat. The result? You can catch fish all year round without really having to consider the weather or the temperature; basically, the fish don't care too much about the conditions and will often feed even if you have to break the ice to get at them. Indeed, trout are more likely to be put off by high water temperatures and bright sunlight – which is convenient because it means you can use those sunny days to relax in a beer garden instead. It's worth noting at this point that trout in particular are bizarre, unpredictable fish – sometimes so canny and skittish that they're impossible to catch, while at other times behaving in the most foolish and unexpectedly gormless manner.

If you need to fish running water for trout and salmon (either to prove a point or because you have a love of heroic failure), then the season is April to October, after which they become more interested in each other than eating and the place turns into a piscine knocking shop. Fishing a top water like the River Test in Hampshire will offer the best chance of catching something worth boasting about, but is fraught with peril – both for your burgeoning reputation as a 'proper' fly fisherman and for your wallet, since a day's fishing costs between £250 and £350 'per rod'. On a prized salmon 'beat' on the Spey or the Tay in Scotland, the cost can be many times more.

But there's a reason that fishermen will pay to fish the best waters. Nothing quite beats the thrill of pursuing the 'king of fish', and salmon fishing is a sport drenched in myth and legend.

The late Paul Torday, author of *Salmon Fishing in the Yemen*, wrote about 'the absolute feeling of peace that comes with fishing as you wade down a pool, concentrating on putting out as good a line as you can. I've fished early in the morning and seen deer swimming the river below me, and the blue flash of a kingfisher. Then there's the adrenalin rush when you hook a salmon in fast water, and have to fight every inch of the way to bring it into the net; or else hook a grilse (a young salmon) that walks across the water on its tail as you play it...'

You probably won't speak of it in quite such dreamlike terms (he was a bestselling writer, after all), but don't lose an opportunity to wax lyrical about fishing whatever water you can afford – like perhaps a classic chalk stream, or going after the ferocious ferox trout in a dark Scottish loch. Allow yourself to affect a certain faraway, misty expression when recalling your finest moments.

When they use words like 'Hairy Mary' or 'jungle muddler', 'humongous' or 'booby', they are referring to flies you might use, rather than you and your appearance.

But back to reality. For the bluffer, there's an obvious choice if you want to catch game fish on the fly. Still-water commercial trout fisheries – sometimes called 'put-and-take' fisheries because they put fish in and you take them out – are the easy favourite. They're much more affordable than most rivers (you'll rarely pay more than £40 for a day's fishing) and you can buy tickets for half a day, a full day or an evening. There's an important point to note here: you must never admit to fishing in one of these places if you want to pass as an expert fly fisherman. But if you want to catch plenty of fish, don't even pause to think. That's where you should go. And should the subject come up, never talk knowledgeably about the growth of dedicated inland salmon lakes in the UK; at last count there was only one.

Most put-and-take lakes have beautifully manicured wide strips of grass round the edges – a bit like a 10-lane running track – without any trees or bushes; this makes it easier to cast because anglers don't have to worry about getting hooked on something or somebody while the line's being flicked behind them.

You'll soon notice that these fisheries have more rules (about fish limits, catch and release, etc.) than a health and safety notice board, and it's important to acquaint yourself with them so as to blend in properly. Every fishery is different, but don't be surprised to see them regularly enforced by roving bailiffs and, in some cases, all-seeing CCTV. Acquaint yourself with these rules or risk being unceremoniously chucked out.

FLY-FISHING BASICS

Reeling 'em in

For a branch of fishing that's so full of complexity and nuance, this part's disarmingly simple; trout bluffers can bring a single rod, reel and line with confidence.

(Remember that it's a '9ft fly rod for a 5-weight line' and pretty much any old fly reel.) As for flies, lures or nymphs, you can always enquire what's fishing well in advance when you book your ticket; this is considered polite, will be accepted as good form, and in no way shows your ignorance. Note: when they reply with words like 'Hairy Mary' or 'jungle muddler', 'humongous' or 'booby', they are referring to flies you might use, rather than you and your appearance.

If you're bluffing about salmon fishing, you might suggest a rather beefier 12- to 13-foot double-hander – because salmon tend to be bigger fish. A 16-footer might be more appropriate if you're fishing with a 'sinking' line.

It is as well to note here the difference between 'dry' and 'wet' fly fishing. It has nothing to do with your political affiliations. Fishing with a dry fly involves keeping it on the surface of the water and imitating insects which are doing the same. A wet fly imitates something moving about beneath the surface (and it needn't necessarily be a 'fly'; it could be designed to resemble anything edible). The effect is achieved by using 'floating' or 'sinking' lines. Comment that you have always found dry fly fishing to be more rewarding because you can claim to have cast it right on the fish's nose and you can see more of what's happening.

The fly is cast
You must prepare for the thorny problem of casting a fly, otherwise your cover will be blown instantly and you'll be exposed for the bluffer you really are. This isn't a how-to guide in the accepted sense, but if you practise

one thing before you expose your 'technique' to other fly fishermen, make sure it's casting. If you remember only one useful tip, make sure it's this: don't overdo the amount of line swirling about behind you and don't let the rod tip bend past the vertical. Actually, that's two tips. Whatever; if it looks like someone's going to question you on your casting knowledge, start using words like 'flex', 'leverage' and 'loop shape'. That should be enough to persuade them to back off.

Why is casting a fly so difficult? Because unlike other styles of fishing, there's no weight at the end of the line to help propel the fly forwards and out into/onto the water. Instead, you use the mainline itself (which is much thicker than 'normal' fishing line) to provide the weight for casting by using a movement not unlike cracking a whip with one hand, while the other strips line off the reel; in this way it's possible to make casts of 30 or 40 yards or more. Of course, if you actually try to fly cast like Indiana Jones, you will likely crack the fly off the end of your line and lose it in a tree somewhere behind you while the mainline pools accusingly at your feet.

Interestingly, while every fly fisher is taught the importance of using the wrist and not the arm with a discipline that recalls learning to fence with an épée, when it actually comes to fly casting in the wild, you'll see all sorts of horrible mash-ups – but if it gets the fly in the water without taking someone's eye out, it's a fly cast. And speaking of taking eyes out, wear a pair of glasses – preferably ones with proper, polarised lenses which cut out surface glare and help you see fish just beneath the surface. They will help you look the part, but they also perform a vital role: anglers lose eyes to badly cast flies every year, from hooks or from the line itself, as it travels at tremendous speed and can be very dangerous.

On the take

When a trout or salmon takes a fly, you'll need to know that it'll either smash into it like an ice-hockey player making a tackle or pick at it like a fussy debutante trying her first Ferrero Rocher – wanting the chocolate without actually wanting to taste it. Your best bet is to watch the line (rather than trying to see the fly) since this will move before you actually feel anything. When you see the line being pulled away, lift the rod in a smooth, deliberate movement – rather than snatching at it – and you should make contact with the fish. The second trick is to try to be aware of where the fly is in relation to the end of the thicker fly line; watch for swirls or flashes near where you think the fly is, because this may be a fish that's taken the fly but is coming towards you and thus not moving the line. Yet.

The play's the thing

In most styles of fishing, you play the fish using the reel – not so with trout and salmon fishing, at least not exclusively so, probably because that would be too simple. Flies are usually worked across the surface or under the water by pulling the line through the rings of the rod using the hand that isn't holding the rod butt, and this movement attracts the fish to the fly. Line pulled in like this collects in a tangled coil around the angler's feet and, when the fly has been retrieved close enough to the bank, you switch over to the reel and wind the rest of the line in. If a fish takes the fly as you're pulling the line in with your other hand, you'll continue to play it using the same technique – partly because you'll never be able to reel in all the line that's on the floor and partly because a tiny fly reel can't keep pace with a fast-moving trout or salmon, especially if it's swimming towards you. The exception to this rule is if you hook a large fish, when the advice is to let it go on a controlled run if possible to take up any loose line and then begin to control it with the reel. Just be careful to avoid a *Some-Mothers-Do-'Ave-'Em* moment, so don't step onto the loops as you're trying to play the fish.

Dispatching your fish

If you have surprised yourself by actually landing a fine specimen from a sustainable source, and you have resolved to keep it, you must know about how to swiftly and humanely dispatch it. After admiring its glistening beauty – its sleek lines, its glinting, intelligent eye, the muscular flexing of its powerful tail fin, the way it shimmers in the sunlight – you will honour one of nature's most wonderful creations by bashing it on the bonce.

The approved and time-honoured method is to use a 'priest' – a short, heavy instrument a bit like a sap that's likely to be made out of brass and is used to administer a couple of sharp whaps to the top of the fish's head above the eyes. The key is to be holding the fish with your other hand while you thump it – don't try to stand it upright on the bank and hit it, or lay it on its side; don't try to hold it by the tail and smack it against a tree; and don't try to skewer its brain with a paring knife or any of that nonsense. Use a priest, like all proper fly fishermen do, and you'll fit right in.

FIVE STORIES YOU SHOULD KEEP UP YOUR SLEEVE

Stalking a brookie
What happened 'There's nothing quite like seeing a fish, stalking it, getting into position, then making the cast. I remember seeing a decent-sized brook trout nosing its way downstream towards where I was standing and putting the fly right on his nose. Took it without hesitation. Gave a decent little scrap, too. Cooked him later with a lemon and almond sauce.'

What actually happened You were about to give up when a particularly stupid trout literally swam into your empty landing net from which you were pretending to release your catch (in case anybody was watching).

Bear necessity
What happened 'I was in Alaska on a remote stretch of the Nushagak, 300 miles west of Anchorage, and I'd hauled in a couple of 20lb king salmon. Just downstream was a bear cub doing a bit of fishing and frolicking. Suddenly I looked up to find a maternally outraged grizzly standing at her full height no further than 10 feet away. We looked at each other for a minute or so until she was momentarily distracted by the cub. There was only one thing to do. I got the bigger of the

salmon out of the landing net and threw it at her. She got it full in the face and boy, was she angry. Fortunately she took it out on the fish, and I just made it back to the jetboat with her in hot pursuit. Started first time and I screamed off, giving her a good dousing.'

What actually happened 'I was fishing with a tour party in the deepest part of the river, rod over the side, when somebody shouted "Grizzly!". I was so frightened I dropped the rod in.'

The marrow spoon
What happened 'Couldn't for the life of me work out what they were taking but I persevered with a March Brown and caught a nice rainbow. Despatched him with the priest and took a marrow spoon to him to see what was going on. Turned out they were gorging themselves on sedges and when I switched to one fish started rising immediately.'

What actually happened Somebody walked past and said: 'I'd still be fishing there at Christmas if I didn't tie on a Green Peter sedge.' It worked.

Take it to the limit
What happened 'There's a two-fish limit on the water so my pals and I (game anglers have pals, coarse anglers have mates, faraway anglers have guides, and sea anglers have no one) just snipped the points off the hooks for the first couple of hours, otherwise we'd have been done and dusted in about half an hour.'

What actually happened You forgot to bring your fly box and it took you two hours to summon the courage to scrounge a fly from someone else.

Perseverance pays off

What happened 'Sometimes you just need to keep at it. Work your way through your fly box, try any pattern you can, no matter how outlandish. I once caught a lake record on a fly so odd-looking that you'd barely credit it as a fly at all.'

What actually happened That's because it was a worm.

FIVE PLACES YOU MUST HAVE FISHED

A brook somewhere

No need to specify where. The point is that it's a tiny stream, only a few inches deep in parts, with tree-lined banks that make it almost impossible to cast. Although many fly anglers never fish anywhere like this (it combines difficult fishing with small fish), they naturally admire those who do.

River Test

Still regarded as England's premier chalk-stream fishery, the Test is the gorgeous, expensive home to some of the country's finest dry fly fishing. Whitchurch Fulling Mill is as good a place as any to reference, wading in the upper section and bank fishing from the lower; it's a top venue for 'sight fishing', where you can see the fish perfectly, and the tail of the mill pool itself holds some really large trout.

River Wharfe

A large river in the Yorkshire Dales, the Wharfe is home to a good head of stocked and wild brown trout. Tell people you went between Sandholme and the Stepping Stones. This 'beat', which is what river fly anglers call a 'swim', is not far from Bolton Abbey and is shadowed by the popular Dales Way. So you can moan about how the rainbow-coloured walking enthusiasts scare the fish down.

Chew Valley Lake

Not far from Bristol, this man-made reservoir was created in 1956 and holds nearly 20 billion litres of water, covers 2,000 acres and has a shoreline of 10 miles. Bang on about how big it is, how you had to fish a floating line with a team of nymphs – heaviest one on the point – and caught a succession of fat stocked trout (don't forget – 'stockies'). Talk knowledgeably about the drowned village of Moreton beneath you (it was mentioned in the Domesday Book).

River Thurso

Close to a private beat favoured by The Queen Mother and Prince Charles, the Thurso in the far north of Scotland has the twin advantages of being, first, a legendary salmon river and, second, very far away. Tell them you fished beat number four with your favourite gnarled old gillie Archie and caught a six-pound salmon that was almost black, then celebrated with a glass of the Lagavulin – this being in the days before the local Wolfburn distillery opened for business again.

ß

"Fish, I love you and respect you very much. But I will kill you dead before this day ends."

(*Ernest Hemingway, The Old Man and the Sea*)

ALL AT SEA

There's no season – and no licence necessary – for sea fishing, so you can go all year round if you want to. Just be sure to wrap up for the cold and take good waterproofs, along with stout boots with excellent grips, or waders with studs on the soles; this is important whether you're fishing from the shore, the rocks or from a boat. In fact, why not go the whole hog and invest in full trawlerman oilskins? You never know what the ocean's going to throw at you. George Clooney sported a good look in the film *The Perfect Storm*, but that might be a bit over the top – especially if you're clutching a thermos behind a windbreak on the beach.

Although many sea fish will feed throughout the year, most are at their best in late summer and autumn, mainly because they've been feeding freely and are nice and fat. That said, there are specific times that are best for particular fish. Winter is good for dab, flounder, whiting and cod; summer and autumn are best for bass, mackerel, dogfish and pollock; while spring offers your best chance of good fishing for pouting and plaice. Avoid bright days; not only is there more chance that the fish can see you, but they're also more visible themselves to airborne predators and, over thousands of years, even mackerel (infamous for their pinhead-sized brains and extraordinary stupidity) have worked out that this is not good for their health. You should avoid strong winds of any description as they are likely to make casting erratic. If fishing from the beach, the best kind of wind is an offshore one which comes from behind you and blows towards the sea.

TIDES OF CHANGE

Unlike freshwater fishing, sea anglers also have to contend with tides. Knowing the basics will impress people who don't. This is all you need to know:

- There's a high tide twice a day and a low tide twice a day. Each day the time of these tides shifts forward by 40 minutes. Seaside local newspapers often carry tide tables, or you can get them from a local tackle shop or find them online.

- You may have heard that tides have something to do with the moon. That's because as the moon orbits the earth it exerts a gravitational pull. Although earth won't budge, water will, and this is what creates a high tide.

- Strong tides are called 'spring tides' and occur when the moon's gravitational pull is at its strongest. Weak tides are called 'neap tides' and...you guessed it.

Tides are important for both fish and anglers, particularly if you're fishing from the shore. Turning up saddled like a pack mule with loads of gear only to discover that it's low tide and the sea is actually half a mile away over claggy sand is no fun; neither is it a good idea to set up camp when the tide is on the turn so you have to keep moving as it chases you back up the beach. Tides are important for fish because they stir things up – everything from plankton to shellfish to crustaceans and little fish – pushing them this way and that. In addition, crabs and worms bury themselves in the sand at low tide and emerge as the tide comes in, bringing a lot of hungry fish with it. If you find yourself on a sandy or a shingle beach, try fishing when the tide is coming in or going out, rather than when it's high or low. If you're fishing off the pier or harbour wall, fish just before, during and after high tide.

SEA OR SHORE?

It is easy to agonise over this (well, not really) because instinctively you will feel that fishing from a boat offers the best chance of catching something, mainly because the most difficult component of the entire exercise – i.e., the finding of the fish – is delegated to someone else: the skipper. This leaves you to bring along some simple tackle, master one or perhaps two techniques, and you're away. You won't even have to cast because the tackle is just lowered over the side of the boat. However, there are several red flags that you'll need to take note of:

1. **Angler proximity alert** You're likely to be stuck, cheek by jowl, with five or six other anglers for hours at a time, all of whom will have doctorates in angling, compared with your solitary, just-scraped GCSE.

2. **Large fish** Find a skipper who knows his stuff and can put you on top of a wreck where conger eel, ling and cod hang out, and there's every chance that you'll catch something decent – 10lb to 15lb or more. Hauling the brute up shouldn't be a problem because sea tackle is pretty stout, but 15lb of angry conger will bang about all over the place, threatening to make a bird's nest of other anglers' lines and causing all manner of problems when you try to actually get it into the boat.

3. **There will be vomit** Sea sickness – the result of the inner ear and the brain bickering over whether you're pitching up and down and side to side or not – is a genuine problem for some people and is completely incompatible with your image as a salty sea dog. Fortunately, there are some useful little pills for this which can be bought over the counter in a pharmacy. If all else fails, keep your eyes firmly fixed on the horizon. It works for some.

Given these caveats, it's worth considering the safest, simplest form of sea fishing – one that even the least sophisticated bluffer will be able to handle with ease. It's called pier fishing – because whether it's a little wooden jetty, a concrete slab where boats are launched, a nice

Victorian fancy on stilts, or an enormous, modern stone structure, if there's one thing you should know about piers – it's that they're easy.

PIER REVIEW

Pier fishing only costs a few pounds per rod for the day. There are no boats; you can drive there or get the bus. You can reel in, leave the rod, and go for a pint or some fish and chips (so if the worst comes to the worst, you can say later in all honesty: 'Yes, I had a nice cod'). You can chat to passers-by about the weather and whether you've caught anything, without ever having to worry about actually catching anything. This is the joy of pier fishing.

The bottom of the sea is like the M25 – featureless, dreary, unchallenging, monotonous, constant and flat, with millions of fish going: 'Are we there yet?'

There are so many people coming and going that you can just blend in; it's like hiding in plain sight. As if that wasn't enough, in addition to people, piers also attract fish. Think about it. The bottom of the sea is like the M25 – featureless, dreary, unchallenging, monotonous, constant, flat, with long, slow bends and millions of fish going: 'Are we there yet?' Then, suddenly, a service station hoves into view with its petrol and bright lights, fast-food outlets and coffee shops, shoals of other fish... Anyway, you get the idea.

A pier is what anglers call a 'feature', and fish love features. Food collects around features, and so do little things that feed on that food, and bigger things that feed on those little things and small fish that feed on them, and bigger fish that are about to feed on them when, what's this? A delicious-looking wriggling something has appeared in front of my mouth. Mmyummmmmm...yank! Because the fish come to you, there's no need to cast. In fact, anglers who cast any distance from the pier are throwing their bait away from the fish (which you might point out to someone wrestling with a reel the size of a barrel and a weight the size of a brick). Instead, make your way to the middle of the pier, note which way the tide is running and, if possible, fish so that your bait will be pulled slightly under the pier when you drop it over the side. You may lose some tackle doing it this way but your bait will be among the fish, whereas if you drop it in the other side, the tide will drag it away from the pier and thus away from the fish. It really is that simple.

WHICH BAIT?

In the main, the kind of fish you're likely to find around a pier don't care very much what they eat. If you need a sense of how intelligent a typical sea fish is, just remember that it's possible to catch mackerel on a piece of silver paper or even a bare hook. As well as all the natural food that accumulates around a pier, people chuck all sorts of stuff in, so the locals have developed pretty catholic tastes. Bread works – so do garden worms and maggots. You can also always find vacuum-packed preserved baits – mackerel strips, squid, sand eels, lug and ragworms and so on – which are okay, too. However, in order to maximise your chances, you're largely better off with fresh lugworms or ragworms which you can buy from a tackle shop. You may stand even more of a chance with squid or peeler crab, but preparing these requires the skills of a medical examiner (step-by-step instructions on how to prepare peeler crab are found easily online but it's like an alien autopsy); you might be able to persuade one of the small, feral children who hang around piers to do it for you. But make it look like you're teaching them, otherwise your credibility will be terminally damaged.

WHICH ROD AND REEL?

For pier fishing you might say that you're better off using a carp rod. Yes; for sea fishing use a rod that's designed to catch a fish that doesn't actually live in the sea, because that's just the way bluffers do things. More seriously, carp rods are really cheap (you can pick one up for a tenner online) and powerful enough to deal with 99% of the fish you're ever likely to catch off the pier. Match it with a cheap carp reel (about the same price), many of which come preloaded with line to get you started.

Again, this book isn't going to get into the nitty-gritty of rigs and techniques, but one thing you will need to consider is what to do with your rod once the bait is in the water. Some anglers use a proper beachcaster tripod, but bluffers should know that many old hands just lean the rod on the pier rail and secure the butt end to something with a bit of bungee cord. Finally, loosen the drag on the reel so that in the event of you hooking something decent, it doesn't drag the rod along the rail or – heaven forbid – into the sea.

BAIT AND WAIT

So, you've found your spot, tackled up, baited up, dropped the whole caboodle over the side and let it sink to the bottom. Now what? You wait, that's what. And if you get a bite, you wait some more. And if you get another bite, you go off for a nice stroll. And if you get another bite, you disappear for a cup of tea. Then, when you come back, you slowly reel in and see what you've caught. That's right. Smart pier anglers don't strike straight away because they invariably fish with more than one hook – often two or three are tied at various points towards the end of the line so you can fish at different depths and catch different species. In this way, you maximise your chances of catching more than one fish at a time and, since most fish caught off the pier are usually quite small (under a pound, say), hooking more than one at a time isn't a problem. As for striking, pier anglers don't – not unless the rod is jerked round or the line suddenly goes slack, both of which are indicators that you've got a larger-than-normal fish on the end.

Since sea tackle is so hefty and the fish you're likely to catch relatively small, you won't have any problems playing them, so just reel in slowly and steadily. Anything of ¾lb and under can just be winched up the side of the pier but, with anything larger, you may need to use a drop net. This is essentially a round, pan-style net on the end of a line. You drop the net into the water, being careful not to hit the fish and knock it off the hook, then manoeuvre it into position and draw the fish over it. Then you pull the net up.

What are you likely to catch off a pier? It depends on different factors but, broadly speaking, expect to catch garfish, mackerel, mullet (if you're lucky), pollock, wrasse, bream, bass (if you're really lucky), whiting, pouting and various flatfish. You can eat all of these fish, with the exception of wrasse.

Speaking of eating your catch, while there are no size limits that dictate which sea fish can be killed and taken home to eat – apart from those that result from common sense – you're legally required to return sea bass under 40cm to the water. Serious anglers are really hot on this stuff so learn to recognise a bass (let the local fishmonger's slab be your bible), take a tape measure with you and act accordingly. Any fish returned to the sea needs to be handled with care. If you're fishing from a pier, for example, handle the fish with a wet (not damp) cloth, pop it back into the drop net and lower it back into the water. Any fish you're going to eat needs to be whacked firmly on the head with a priest (*see* page 79).

SOME BACKSTORY

Of course, pier fishing is only a tiny part of the sea-fishing story, so if you find yourself metaphorically lost at sea with a bunch of anglers who are starting to query your credentials, keep in mind the following stories to help you find your way back to shore and safety.

FIVE STORIES YOU SHOULD KEEP UP YOUR SLEEVE

The conger in the boat
What happened 'Last cast of the night. Sea like a millpond and a sliver of moon riding above and I hooked into this enormous conger eel. Took 20 minutes to get it up and into the boat and it thrashed around so hard that it knocked one of the guys over. Cracked his head on the side of the cabin. Thought he was a goner. That conger was a brute.'

What actually happened You slipped on a bit of squid mantle (the bell-shaped bit) that was being used as bait and went arse over tit.

Mullet, mullet everywhere
What happened 'Well, you know how notoriously hard to catch they are; I couldn't believe it. Found a shoal in the estuary over at (insert name of local river here) and they were mad for it. Fished bread flake under a little waggler float and caught six in six casts. Kept topping the swim up with handfuls of mashed bread. The place was mullet-crazy.'

What actually happened You went to a 1980s-themed weekend at Butlins.

Trapped on the rocks
What happened 'I'd been put onto this great mark for pollock on the headland. Stupidly, I didn't realise that it was a spring tide and when the water came in, it looked as though I was going to be cut off. That's when your experience kicks in. I picked my way back across the rocks – which were razor sharp – and jumped the last gap, just as the water was rushing in. Cut my foot but, otherwise, no harm done. It's always important to treat the sea with respect.'

What actually happened Your flip-flops got washed out to sea while you were having a paddle and you had to walk back across a shingle beach in your bare feet. Now your feet hurt.

Monsters of the deep
What happened 'The skipper put us over the wreck and we dropped the baits. As we drifted down I got an extraordinary take that nearly bent the rod in half. I fought it for nearly 15 minutes when the line just parted. Until then I'd pumped the rod up, then down, then up, as the fish and I sort of took turns, each pulling the other. I don't know what it was – a big ray, maybe?'

What actually happened Failing to control your tackle properly, your rig got tangled with someone else's line on the opposite side of the boat. The pair of you seesawed back and forth for a bit while the skipper wet himself laughing.

Some beautiful bass
What happened 'Got into some of the most fantastic bass of my life. It was like a blur.'

What actually happened You drank a lot of draught Bass. After that, everything was a blur.

FIVE PLACES YOU SHOULD HAVE FISHED
Given that Britain's coastline is about 11,000 miles, there are plenty of places to fish, either from the shore or out on a boat. Even the keenest angler can't have fished everywhere, so here are a few key locations – or 'marks', as sea anglers like to call them – for you to drop into the conversation.

Chesil Beach
Ah, the famous shingle beach that runs from Portland in the south up to West Bay in the, er…west. At its best from May through to September, the steeply shelving beach attracts large fish of many species, but particularly cod and bass. Tell them you went at the end of August on a hot summer's evening and caught trigger fish up to 3lb. Make a point of saying how bad-tempered they were when you unhooked them.

The Muchalls
Just north of Stonehaven in Aberdeenshire, in the shadow of the Old Man of Muchalls, lies a mark famous for

producing large cod. Say that the best place to park is near Doonie Point, and make your way down to the water from there. The tide is fierce, the rocks are treacherous (the area is popular with local rock climbers) but the rewards are great – fine fishing set against magnificent scenery.

Whitby wreck fishing

The mecca of cod fishing – this is where the British record 58-pounder was caught in 1992. Say that you went out with a great skipper who put you right on top of the fish. You had cod all day, a few into double figures, most on peeler crab, but a few of the bigger ones on peeler and white-rag cocktail. Fantastic.

Porth Joke

Just four miles from Newquay centre on the north coast of Cornwall, make sure you refer to this secluded cove as 'Polly Joke', which is what the locals call it. What makes it special is the scenery and – especially out of holiday season – the peace and quiet. No Mr Whippy vans means no grubby children smeared in ice cream running around disturbing your fishing.

Herne Bay Harbour Arm

When the water's really clear, seek out the elusive mullet by fishing on the inside with a light rod and bread flake under a small float. Most people make the mistake of heading towards the end of the arm but you will know that the best fishing is nearer the car park and in the middle section. It's also one of the best places to catch large whiting in the whole of Kent.

ß

Knowing how to handle a beachcaster doesn't mean you're even remotely prepared to catch something that's as big as you are.

WORLD OF SPORT

Exotic fishing encompasses many different styles of angling – some of which you'll already be familiar with if you've read the preceding chapters. Sport fishing is as diverse as there are fish in the sea. Think that's an exaggeration? Consider, then, that in and around the Maldives alone – one of the most popular destinations in the world for sport fishing – there are more than 1,000 different kinds of fish that you can catch, from small, multi-coloured parrotfish right up to the mighty ball-breaking sailfish which can weigh over 100kg.

No matter what anglers say ('I'm happy to catch anything' or 'It's not the actual fish that matter; it's the experience of being close to nature' and other bunkum), there are certain totem fish that have more gravity and carry more weight (not always literally) and would sit near the top of most anglers' lists. These fish are Chelsea or Arsenal rather than Swindon or Yeovil Town; they are The Beatles and The Rolling Stones rather than Bucks Fizz or The Dave Clark Five; a 16-year-old Lagavulin, not a two-litre bottle of White Lightning.

Sport fishing involves chasing totem fish all over the world, allowing you to gather some useful anecdotal ammunition along the way with which to convince the doubters that you've pursued your elusive quarry to the literal ends of the earth and emerged triumphant, trophy in hand. Naturally, this is then captured by camera and lovingly massaged by Photoshop to produce a genuine digitally enhanced record of man's triumph over fish.

GENERAL ADVICE

Despite the fact that you'd think that anyone who pays thousands of pounds to go fishing halfway across the world will know what they're doing, this is not necessarily the case. This is good news for bluffers. Remember:

- Everyone, even the most experienced angler, is likely to be out of their comfort zone. Even those in your party who've been before and consider themselves old hands will remember what it was like the first time and are usually keen to help, or at least show off.

- Knowing how to handle a beachcaster doesn't mean you're even remotely prepared to catch something that's as big as you are.

- Skippers and guides will put you where the fish are because it's their job and they want you to come back next year.

- Given half a chance, eager-to-please guides will do the difficult bits for you – preparing the rig, baiting up, casting, striking, even helping to play the fish in certain circumstances. This is all fine; lean back in a lordly way and let them.

- Stick with official guides rather than being tempted off-piste by someone you met in a beach bar after too much Mekong whisky.

- The usual – get your jabs, take anti-malaria pills where necessary, only drink bottled water, wear a hat, use sunblock and don't tease the stingrays...

TOTEM FISH

Taimen
Though the name may conjure visions of a race of fierce Scottish cousins to Frank Herbert's desert-dwelling Fremen, these are actually a species of salmon which are found in the huge, fast-flowing rivers of Outer Mongolia. No, that's not a euphemism. Taimen hang out in northern Mongolia, which means you have to as well. This is no easy task. You'll fly into Chinggis Khaan International Airport (yep, named after the very same well-known thirteenth-century liberal statesman) in the capital Ulaanbaatar, and from there it's either a helicopter ride or hard day's drive over the steppe to one of the camps that nestle along Mongolia's mighty taimen rivers which have names – Eg and Uur – that sound like someone clearing their throat.

Best fished for between June and October, taimen are giant salmon that can grow to 60lb, live more than 50 years, and spend most of their lives in fresh water looking for a fight. Famed for their aggression and the savage way they 'hit' a lure or fly, you must never try to take a taimen home for your tea – indeed, most guides insist that they're not removed from the water, which is why in almost every photo you see of angler and taimen, the former is up to his waist in water looking more than apprehensive as he holds a distinctly peevish-looking monster of a fish. Tip: be very careful.

Mahseer

Take a carp, armour-plate it and then increase its size to, oh, say 80lb, add a massive spade-like tail and teach it to swim at 20 knots; then put it in the Cauvery River in India (all rocks and froth) and invite foreigners to try to catch it without getting pulled in. The mahseer fishing industry is one of the best developed in the world, with some of the most experienced guides and tour operators. Yet, because it happens in India, there's a happy unpredictability to proceedings, which usually adds a frisson for Europeans who are used to itineraries that run in more linear fashion.

Tackle is rarely supplied, but even basic camps without electricity are comfortable, while some of the permanent ones are really fancy, with ice-cold Kingfisher beer and first-class local grub. Use clear or green 40lb-breaking-strain line and fish with a large ball of ragi paste – millet mixed with spices and water. And we mean large. Think of an orange and you're in the right ballpark. Guides will put you close to the fish and will often cast for you – more important, they'll be on hand to laugh at you when you're playing the fish and to help you land it. For some reason, the sight of prosperous Western folk scrambling over massive, sharp rocks while the river rages below and a huge mahseer tears off into the distance is endlessly amusing.

Bonefish

While most sport fish are goliaths, mighty and intimidating, bonefish are like goblins or velociraptors – fast, mean and toothsome. They hang around in small groups on large, shallow mudflats, waiting for the tide to bring in their breakfast, like teenagers lurking outside McDonald's looking for an easy meal. Where it's allowed, you fly fish for them, wading out to your thighs in lovely, warm water, and fish by sight – looking for a telltale shadow just beneath the surface and then casting to it. Polarised glasses are essential for cutting out some of the glare, and you'll need to be able to cast a fly at least 20 feet in order to stand a chance. Typical bonefish aren't big – you can usually hold them in one hand – but because the water is so shallow, they've got nowhere to dive so tear off sideways, stripping line from your reel as they go.

Fortunately for fishermen, bonefish make their home in some of the loveliest parts of the planet – the Bahamas is a popular destination – though this does tend to send the price for a holiday through the roof. You can expect to pay £3,000 or more for a seven-day trip which may only feature four days of fishing. Go between November and June and you'll be in for some fun; bonefish fight like weasels who've been drinking jet propellant. Say that you relish the challenge.

Giant trevally

The giant trevally – or 'GT' as it's known – is an astonishingly vicious, broad-shouldered brute that grows to 200lb and looks like an enormous piranha with shark fins. God help any angler who hooks one; even a small GT will provide the kind of scrap you usually associate with a bare-knuckle brawl. Found in the tropical waters of the Indian and Pacific Oceans, particularly around the Hawaiian archipelago, they travel in small packs, like wolves, and when they attack a shoal of bait fish, they do so with such ferocity that the smaller fish float stunned to the surface where they can be picked off at the trevally's leisure. They can be caught relatively near the shore, which obviates the need for expensive, boring trips with other anglers, and they respond well to lures, especially poppers which make a lot of ruckus on the surface, and stickbaits which can also be worked just underneath; either way, be prepared for a monster hit when one takes the bait. If you have a death wish you can also fly fish for them, but remember that when Ash, the robot in *Alien*, describes the xenomorph thus: 'Perfect organism. Its structural perfection is matched only by its hostility,' he's actually talking about a GT. You have been warned. But if you insist, claim to have fought one close to submission and then released it as an acknowledgment of its warrior-like nobility. When asked how you got close enough to unhook it, gaze stoically into the far distance and say that the wounds took a long time to heal.

> When asked how you got close
> enough to unhook it, gaze stoically
> into the far distance and say that the
> wounds took a long time to heal.

White sturgeon

Canada's Fraser River is the place to go for these behemoths which can grow to over 1,000lb and look as though they've been carved from soapstone. Don't claim to have caught one this big – not least because you'd need a twin-engined Caterpillar to haul it ashore. Claim that 100lb to 200lb is a more typical size, but 'even they will give you the scrap of a lifetime'. Being Canada, it's all terribly organised. Fish are protected (and thus plentiful), tours are guided, and everyone speaks English – even if it is with some funny intonations, eh? The face of a sturgeon is like a tiny-eyed, dopey shark wearing a set of false whiskers (these are sensitive barbules which feel for food along the bottom of the river), but the fish's colouring and markings are magnificent. A great fish to go after, thanks to the frosty Canadian beer and high levels of mollycoddling involved.

Blue marlin

The classic sport fish, with its distinctive, spear-like snout and massive, ridged, sail-like dorsal fin, which is often played while the angler is seated strapped to a 'fighting chair'. Of course, many modern anglers may be hefty enough to think they can hold their own, even against fish that grow to over 1,000lb and are able to leap entirely clear of the water in their efforts to escape. They're wrong. Try somewhere like Florida which is relatively cheap to get to and has plenty of other activities for anyone who needs time to recharge their engines. This isn't hyperbole; a fight with a blue marlin can take several hours, and since most visitors 'train' on pizza and beer, the fish is certainly going to be in better shape than the angler who's trying to catch it.

Nile perch
Head to Lake Nasser in Egypt, an artificially created lake where these large and powerful predators – say 200lb and counting – are waiting to tear the lures off the end of any line dropped into the water by an unsuspecting angler. Nile perch are bizarre creatures, resembling small fish that have been zapped by a *Honey-I-Blew-Up-The-Kids* ray gun until they reach monstrous proportions. Guided tours scour the lake, find the fish for you using sonar (a necessity, this; there's over 2,000 square miles of water to search) and in a quaint, science-fiction touch, all the little fishing boats return to a mother ship at night so you can get a decent meal and a comfy bed for the night.

Great White Shark
Don't. They're endangered (along with many other shark species). And, anyway, you wouldn't want to end up like Captain Quint in *Jaws*, would you?

POPULAR AQUA-CULTURE

Although many anglers point to four-time world champion Bob Nudd's novelty single 'Maggots in Ya Catapult' ('I'm comin' atcha/gonna hit you like a thunderbolt/groundbait, casters, maggots in your catapult') as the zenith of angling poetry, the sport has actually produced or inspired a wide oeuvre in the arts, popular culture and the world of entertainment. No sniggering at the back.

There are many famous anglers, of course, some of whom – like Jack Charlton, Billy Connolly and Chris Tarrant – people know about, and others – Roger Daltrey, Liam Neeson, Jeremy Paxman, Eric Clapton, Jane (*Dr Quinn, Medicine Woman*) Seymour, Tiger Woods, Bing Crosby and American presidents Bush, Nixon and Carter – that they might not; heck, even the notoriously attention-challenged Paul Gascoigne goes fishing.

So, since referencing popular culture and the arts is always useful to give a bluffer some context and background (a bit of meat on the bluffing bone), it is appropriate to conclude this guide with a whistle-stop tour of some of the conversation-droppers that will help to cement your status as a bona fide 'thinker' about fishing.

LITERATURE

Angling books divide themselves neatly into two types: the practical, hands-on, how-to guides, and the memoirs. In the past, some authors have managed to combine the two, but, in the main, anglers find it hard to string two sentences together, which means that the books are often tedious do-this-then-do-that instructionals. However, you should have at least a passing acquaintance with:

THE COMPLEAT ANGLER
by Izaak Walton (1653)
The original angling book is a dialogue between sporting types full of practical tips and country wisdom (some of which is less relevant today: 'Hie thee to an apothecary' – that kind of thing). Few anglers have ever read it from cover to cover and neither should you. Merely observe that it proves angling is 'the contemplative man's recreation,' then slip away to the bar.

STILLWATER ANGLING
by Richard Walker (1953)
The man who did more than anyone else to convince anglers it was possible to fish – with success – for a particular species, rather than simply putting the hours in and trusting to luck. Bluffer's key facts: he invented the Mark IV carp rod and the electronic bite alarm.

FISHING WITH MR CRABTREE IN ALL WATERS
by Bernard Venables (1964)

Bluffers may even fancy reading this since, in the main, it's a collection of comic strips from the *Daily Mirror*. There's a lot of pipe smoking, trilby hats and short trousers (these are worn by Crabtree's son Peter, rather than the great man himself), and plenty of fish. Seminal for any angler who was growing up in the 1960s and 1970s and surprisingly relevant to this day.

FRESHWATER FISHING
by Fred Buller and Hugh Falkus (1975)

This encyclopedia of fishy facts, angling tactics and – take that, Hugh Fearnley-Whittingstall – recipes should find a place on every bluffer's bookshelf. Like the Bible, in that it's so big that you can open it at random and find something that sounds scarily impressive, and it's often found at a knock-down price in bookshops.

CASTING AT THE SUN
by Chris Yates (1986)

While the 1970s found most young men where they were supposed to be – listening to Pink Floyd in bedrooms and smoking funny cigarettes – Yates and his pals embarked on a series of punishing fishing expeditions for carp. While their contemporaries had the munchies, these obsessives routinely went hungry because they'd spent all their money going fishing – managing to recoup some of their expenses by publishing their experiences a decade later.

FLY FISHING
by JR Hartley

A book that was never actually published in the accepted sense but which nonetheless became one of the most famous written works on fishing in the late twentieth century – except that it was never actually 'written' in the accepted sense either. The 'book' was featured in a 1980s TV advertisement showing a mournful old chap asking for it in several second-hand bookshops. His efforts fail until he resorts to the Yellow Pages, ultimately finds a copy of the book, and asks the shop to keep it for him (this was before the advent of the Internet). Asked for his name, he replies slowly and deliberately: 'JR Hartley'. Stirring stuff, and every bluffer should know about it. And hats off to an entrepreneurial writer called Michael Russell who subsequently wrote a bestselling book called *Fly Fishing, Memories of Angling Days,* by JR Hartley (1991), and a sequel *JR Hartley Casts Again: More Memories of Angling Days* (1992). Some might call it 'cashing in', but not a bluffer.

TV

Angling on TV is usually a hideous affair, thanks to cheap production values and the inability of anglers or fish to do as they're told; anglers routinely explain things with their back to the camera and fish simply don't care. Over the years, however, there have been some notable exceptions which are worth namechecking.

Out Of Town

Fronted by avuncular, pipe-smoking Jack Hargreaves from a fake shed, the series was initially commissioned to look at rural life for six episodes in 1963, but ended up running for 28 years. In the early days, TV was a wasteland as far as fishing was concerned, and Hargreaves proved a perfect presenter – always interesting and interested, a skilful angler, too. Oddly sinister theme music, though.

The Fishing Race

Curious 1976 teatime treat which involved several teams of anglers competing to see who could catch the most different fish in 72 hours. Bad-tempered anglers were seen openly cheating, sabotaging and, in one memorable scene, stealing into an aquarium to catch a piranha. The sequel featured a prank where two anglers were deliberately put off their fishing by the appearance of a topless model in a canoe who'd been hired by an opposing team.

Go Fishing with John Wilson

An ex-hairdresser, beaming beardie and Norwich-based tackle-shop owner, Wilson kept angling on the telly almost single-handedly during the late 1980s and early 1990s, and many thousands of anglers have cause to remember his boisterous, honking delivery. He was a machine when it came to catching fish, though.

A Passion For Angling

On the surface, it was that rarity: a well-paced, beautifully shot, genuinely enjoyable series following two eccentric anglers – Bob James and Chris Yates – as they fished through the seasons. Behind those idyllic six episodes, though, lay four long years of filming. Four endless, grinding years.

Fishing in the Footsteps of Mr Crabtree
An attempt to recreate Bernard Venables' celebrated series of angling cartoon strips (*see* earlier in chapter) on TV in 2013. Fronted by angling author John Bailey, each episode introduced a different 'yoof' to a style of fishing and species of fish. Tried hard to be charming but was oddly stilted.

Other TV anglers worth a mention include Matt Hayes (enthusiastic but a bit process-driven; big hands); Martin Bowler (surely a prog-rock fan with that hair); Jeremy Wade (looks tougher than the river monsters he catches); Keith Arthur (teeth like tombstones – chatty but still surprisingly relevant); and ROBSON GREEN! (shouts a lot; sings even more; fancies himself as a bit of a looker and likes to be thought of as an extreme angler).

THE SILVER SCREEN

Actual angling and action do not great bedfellows make, so most films that feature the sport tend towards the comedic or the contemplative. Of course, there are plenty of movies where fish are cast as the villains – scaly scoundrels in need of aquatic anger management – but there's more to fishing movies than tearing people's arms off.

Jaws (1975)

Everyone's favourite monster fishing film, featuring aquaphobe Roy Scheider, marine biologist Richard Dreyfuss and Robert Shaw as Quint, the mad-as-a-meat-axe captain. Plenty of good quotes, including: 'Here's to swimming with bow-legged women,' which makes a handy toast, and the ever popular – and apparently improvised – 'You're gonna need a bigger boat.'

A River Runs Through It (1992)

Amazingly, angling stays central to this Robert Redford directed adaptation of Norman Maclean's beautiful, bitter novel of a father and his sons. Rather than being relegated to the occasional scene-setting colour, the characters fish all the time and, when they're not fishing, they talk about it. Hell, Brad Pitt even looks like he knows how to cast a fly – which is probably more than you do.

The Old Man and the Sea (1958)

Spencer Tracy's remarkable turn in Hemingway's parable of the sea is always worth referencing. Is he an old man? Is he the sea? Is he really the fish? Is the fish actually the old man? Is the fish really there? And will he put it back?

On Golden Pond (1981)

Henry Fonda may have deserved an Oscar for his turn as the irascible Norman Thayer, but the fishing is a disgrace, especially the scene where he nabs a big rainbow trout and ends up – schoolboy error – with the rod so low that it's pointing at the fish. Even the trout looked embarrassed.

The Perfect Storm (2000)

You know what's going to happen, George Clooney and Mark Wahlberg know what's going to happen, even the fish know what's going to happen. There's a 'perfect' storm, and guess what happens to their trawler? Don't watch if you have a phobia about really big waves.

Salmon Fishing in the Yemen (2011)

Ewan McGregor's presence as the repressed but oddly attractive fisheries scientist ensures that this is one fishing film that strikes a chord with the opposite sex. Tease them with its transformational themes and before you know it – bang, they're hooked!

"Don't tell fish stories where the people know you; but particularly, don't tell them where they know the fish."

Mark Twain

There's no point in pretending that you know everything about fishing – nobody does – but if you've got this far and you've absorbed at least a modicum of the information and advice contained within these pages, then you will almost certainly know more than 99% of the rest of the human race about what fishing is, why people enjoy it, and how you can pretend to be better at it than you are. What you now do with this information is up to you, but here's a suggestion: be confident about your newfound knowledge, see how far it takes you, but above all, have fun using it. You are now a fully fledged expert in the art of angling, one of humankind's oldest, noblest and most addictive pursuits. So go forth and fish.

Oh, and never, ever, put maggots in your mouth to warm them up and make them wriggle on a winter's day. It works but, by God, you'll wish you hadn't...

GLOSSARY

Bait dropper A little cage filled with bait – say, maggots or chopped worms – that is attached to the line and then lowered into the water where you're fishing. As it hits the bottom, the cage opens and releases the bait. Also sometimes refers to a clumsy angler.

Baiting needle Used for poking holes through bait in order to thread line through them. Also used for baiting fellow anglers when you get bored (which is quite often).

Beat What game fishermen call a 'swim' – a spot in which to fish.

Bite alarm Fiendish electronic device designed to rouse an angler from deepest sleep or beer-induced coma; indicates a fish is making off with the bait.

Bivvy Small, domed tent used to ward off the weather during long fishing sessions, during which time its character changes to reflect that of the occupant; some anglers keep everything shipshape and Bristol fashion, while others initiate a dirty protest almost immediately.

Blank When you go fishing and don't catch anything. Also, the look on an angler's face when you ask the question: 'Caught anything?'

Boilies Artificial baits stuffed with flavour enhancers and attractants, originally intended to catch carp but now used for many fish; high fat and protein content said to be responsible for the large bellies seen on modern fish. Anglers should not snack on these while waiting for a bite but, from the looks of their own bellies, many of them do.

Coarse fishing 'Cos you is common, innit? (Alternatively, 'Are you one of those frightful plebs who only fishes still water?')

Commercial fishery Not a lake that has advertising billboards round the edges (though God knows that can't be far away) but one that's managed and stocked regularly with fast-growing fish (known as 'stockies').

Day ticket Unlike Willy Wonka's ticket, this does not allow you entry to a land of chocolate wonder – rather, to a fishery that may or may not contain fish.

Disgorger A thin metal or plastic tool for removing a hook from deep in the mouth of a fish. Also, what a sea angler does during a force 10.

End tackle The stuff that goes at the end of the line, nearest the fish. May include one or more hooks, weights, a single larger weight, swivels, plastic stoppers, a float and so on. Always invites a double entendre.

F1 Cross between crucian and common carp, bred especially for commercial fisheries because they don't grow too big, feed all year round and are highly resistant to disease. Nothing to do with tedious motor sport.

Float fishing Popular style of angling where the end tackle and bait are suspended beneath a float which stands upright in the water; when a fish takes the bait it bobs, then disappears, affording the angler a sensation of something close to a state of absolute bliss.

Game fishing Because you need to be game to spend all that money without catching anything.

Gozzers Home-bred maggots which are larger and whiter than shop-bought ones. Best method is to get a pig's or lamb's heart from the butcher and leave it in a dark, moist place for a week or so. It doesn't bear thinking about.

Hairy Mary One of many evocative names for fishing flies. Others include the Flaming Booby and the Fly Formerly Known as Prince.

Ledgering Style of fishing where the angler uses a weight to cast and keep the bait on the bottom. Bites are usually indicated when the tip of the rod taps or tugs round or when an electronic bite alarm sounds. Not exactly riveting.

Licence fee If you fish in England, you need one of these; watch out for the Fishing Licence detector vans if you haven't bought one.

Lough/loch/lake Irish/Scottish/English name for a large body of still water. The style of fishing most anglers prefer.

Lugworm Unpleasant-looking worm used for sea fishing. The further away from you, the better.

Lure Anything designed to look like a little fish and attract the attentions of a bigger, predatory fish. What tackle dealers do to get anglers into their shops with assurances of free local advice about what to fish, where.

Mark What sea anglers call a 'swim'. What tackle dealers call a customer.

Marrow spoon Long, thin, pen-like instrument for removing the contents of a trout's stomach to see what it's been eating. Not for the squeamish.

Permit Written permission to fish in a particular spot on a particular day. Also aggressive pack fish that live in shallow, tropical waters.

PETA People for the Ethical Treatment of Animals. US-based pressure group which doesn't much like angling and anglers, or anything to do with hunting, shooting or people who wear fur. If it could just focus on where the real cruelty lies, like animal transportation and slaughter, they might persuade a few million anglers to join up.

Pinkies The larvae of the greenfly; fish are very partial to these. (Not to be confused with hairless, newborn mice which are fed to pet lizards and snakes. Fish with those and you really will have PETA after you.)

Playing a fish Most people can't get an actual tune out of a fish, so instead use this phrase to describe the process of extracting the fish from its watery lair.

Poppers A type of lure designed to mimic a small fish thrashing on the surface and not what you were thinking at all.

PVA bag Substance called polyvinyl alcohol which can be made into little bags which dissolve on contact with water. Fill these full of bait, tie near the hook, cast out; PVA disappears, leaving mound of tasty morsels to attract passing fish.

Ragworm Unpleasant-looking worm used for sea fishing that also has – oh, joy – pincers that can give the unwary angler a nasty nip.

Scale-perfect Used to describe a fish that looks like it's never been caught. Substitute with 'pristine' or 'untouched'.

Shot Small weights that look like tiny Pacmen which are pinched onto the line to keep bait on the bottom, balance a float and so on.

Spinning Style of fishing which involves casting and then retrieving a lure in such a way as to make it look like a sickly fish in order to attract larger, hungry fish after an easy meal.

Stickbait A lure that looks like a stick. Don't ask why fish find these interesting.

Striking The act of lifting the rod to set the hook in a fish when you've had a bite.

Swim A fishing spot. What sea anglers call a 'mark' and game anglers call a 'beat'. And what all anglers try to do when they fall in.

Tackle Fishing gear. Don't even think about any other definition.

Waders Extra long rubber boots. Tend to fill with water when you fall in rendering it impossible to swim.

Water What anglers call a place to fish. Also the 'sine qua non' of all piscine life.

A BIT MORE BLUFFING...

Available from all good bookshops

bluffers.com